PULP ERA WRITING TIPS

TABLE OF CONTENTS

Introduction...1

Third Rung from the Bottom...............................2

A Fiction Formula That Helped Me Sell 1,000 Stories...9

A Very Simple System..22

The Requisites for Success..................................29

Breath of Life..32

Butch and His Big Ears......................................37

It's All A Matter of Timing................................44

Get That Novel Out of Your System....................52

Plotting the Short-Story....................................61

How to Write a Fight Sequence..........................107

Let Yourself Go...112

How to Revise a Novel.......................................119

Try Wishful Thinking!.......................................131

How to Write Love Scenes..................................136

How to Write True Detective Mysteries..............145

Why Aren't Your Detective Stories Selling?..........157

Is the Attic Trunk Your Goal?............................167

About the Editor...170

INTRODUCTION

Pretty much everybody who knows me knows that I love the pulp era. Many of my favorite stories were written then. From *Doc Savage* to *The Shadow* to the wildly imaginative stories in *Fantastic Adventures* and *Weird Tales*, I just can't get enough of them.

And when I read *A Princess of Mars* by Edgar Rice Burroughs, well, that's when I knew I wanted to write, too.

Since that time, I've written and I've studied writing and I've written some more. And somewhere along the line, I asked myself, "How did those pulp folks learn to write?" That led me down a pretty deep rabbit hole.

If you've ever been interested in writing pulp at all, chances are that you've read *Lester Dent's Pulp Paper Master Fiction Plot*. It was certainly one of the first things I found. It's a great formula mixed with a pile of helpful tips, and can be used to help crank out a lot of fun short stories. However, that one plot formula is not the only thing there is to know about writing. I wanted more.

Of course, the more I searched online, the more I knew had to be out there *somewhere*. And so began my hobby of buying vintage writing magazines. I've amassed a nice little stack. I thought it might be nice to share, so I've scanned and transcribed and scanned and transcribed some more. Finally, I have collected some of the best articles here.

All of these articles come from issues of publications that are now in the public domain. Some of them feel quite dated, and some of them feel like could have been posted to a writing blog yesterday. I think there is something to be learned from all of them, though, and you'll see a thought or two of mine after each one.

Third Rung from the Bottom

by Evis Joberg

This article originally appeared in the April 1946 Issue of Writer's Digest. This author is one more who has been mostly lost to history. There are a couple of listings for copies of romance novels she wrote, but that's about it.

I wrote my first story when I was nine. I was a skinny, unattractive child with too-big eyes and a pigtail that looked like it weighed more than the rest of me. On top of that, my farmer parents, who were Norwegian immigrants and the salt of the earth, had a joint inferiority complex of gargantuan proportions, which they passed on to me intact. So one day in school I looked at the clean backs of my arithmetic papers and thought with native thriftiness that it was a shame to throw them away. That was the moment when it started, this incurable itch to put words on paper, for I thought, "If I used this paper to write a story, I could write about a girl like me, and make it come out right."

So I wrote a story about a girl who was snubbed by her mates, who, at a picnic, rescued a drowning baby and forthwith became a heroine, admired by her elders and sought after by her contemporaries. I have since learned that, for me at least, the best writing comes out of frustration always. I have also learned that most of the elements of a good story were present in that yarn. I gave it to my teacher to read, for I discovered that it wasn't enough to write for myself; I wanted a reader. She handed it back to me a few days later with errors in spelling and punctuation carefully marked, but without comment. It was, I suppose, my first rejection slip, and it left me puzzled, but not too hurt; for I had had pleasure in the writing. That, too, has stood me in good stead. I wrote a couple more for the same reason. I wish I had kept them.

But the first story I wrote to sell came much later. I had left the farm and gone to the city, which was the fulfillment of one of my little-girl dreams. I got a job, and immediately began to live life, instead of reading about it in books, which was a far healthier thing to do and lots more fun.

After three or four years of having a most marvelous time I married Prince Charming himself, and promptly went to work on a Small Image. The Prince was a Merchant Seaman, away for weeks at a time; so I had lots of time to rediscover the fun of reading. One day I read a confession magazine. There was a contest; "stories out of your own life," it said, and hand-written scripts were acceptable. (I didn't type.) So I wrote a story which I fancied was much like the ones I had read in the magazine, only better, about the kind of people I wished I knew but didn't. When it came back (with speed and a printed rejection slip), I felt, only astonishment. (Clearly there had been a slip-up.) I wrote another ditto. Results were also ditto. Annoyed, I repeated. So did they. Then I climbed the first rung of the writer's ladder. I realized that writing was a business, that it apparently followed rules of some sort; and I discovered *Writer's Digest*.

Eventually, between babies and housework and visits home by the Prince, I began to write again. But with a difference. Now I tried to write what some editor might want. I switched to love stories because I felt that I knew enough about that subject at least to write without pulling any boners. I aimed at the pulps, because the agents with whom I was experimenting seemed to consider them easier to hit. I learned to use a typewriter. And I wrote and wrote. I was climbing the second rung of the ladder: learning the feel of words, learning my own limitations, getting the rudiments of technique. Eventually I settled with one agent; before long he sold a couple of my love pulps. I had already- sold a few articles.

By this time the images had multiplied to three. The Prince had "swallowed the anchor" to our mutual delight, and was now a real, sure-enough husband; coming home to dinner every night. We moved from Seattle to San Francisco, and once more I had the time of my life just having fun. A year whistled by in which I read WD faithfully but wrote not at all. Notice in the Forum department of a Writer's Workshop attracted me, and I went, I listened, and then again-I wrote.

And I climbed up to rung three. Rung one had knocked the nonsense out of me. Rung two had given me a general knowledge of the materials with which I proposed to work, and my own particular shortcomings in handling those materials. It had also given me a little self-confidence. Now, at rung three, I have settled down to learn my job-to learn how to write.

I have often wished that WD would imitate the editors of some of the pulps in putting out an annual, apart from the Year Book, in which they would reprint the best of articles appearing in the preceding year. I should like to make a lot of nominations for that book. Among the ones I would like to see reprinted are-no, on second thought I'm not going to list them, because if you don't have access to those issues it'll only make you mad, and if you have, you won't forget em anyway. But out of the two dozen or so that have really clicked with me, I have evolved a method of working and studying which is paying dividends to me, and which gives me that necessary assurance that I am accomplishing something in the hours I steal for writing. My own plan has four sections. Maybe they will help you.

First. Study. I used to read that word and wonder in anguish, "Sure, study, but how? What shall I look for? How does one study a published story?" Well, I've found some things that help me really learn from the stories I read. None of these, I hasten to add, are original with me; they are composites of the helpful articles I've read, and advice generously handed me by professionals and others.

Take openings, for example. I read the first paragraph or two of a new story. Then I stop and ask myself, what is the mood of this story going to be? How do I know? How much information do I now have concerning the characters, story problem, locale? Which words gave me that information? I've learned plenty from this study. Had you ever noticed, for instance, how many of the best stories open with a sentence which gives you the feeling that you are cutting in on a scene which is already in progress?

"He angled his car into Laurie's driveway, cut the engine, and sat motionless, his hands relaxed on the wheel." So begins "*Pink Dust*," by Marian Sims in March *American.* You cut into the scene where he is reaching the end of a drive; you are immediately concerned with trying to fill in what has gone before, in what is already, occurring. Action! "He raised his hand to knock at the heavy door, but it flew open in his face and a woman's untidy head was thrust around it." He is already on the porch when we see him. The play is under way.

Another hint that has paid off under the heading of study goes like this. Taking four pencils with different colored leads, I begin to re-read a story I enjoyed. All action words are underlined with red; direct description with green; conversation with purple; and narration with yellow. Every word in the story is underlined with the proper color; some of them with two colors. This study will probably amaze you as much as it did me. Which of the four do you think predominates? Try it and see!

Often the thing that keeps my story from selling is not the idea or the plot, but my handling of it. This was made painfully clear to me some months ago when I wrote what I knew should be a good story, only to find it unsalable. A friend who is a professional took the same plot, wrote it up (with my permission, of course), and sold it first trip out for $650.00. He gave me a percentage on the sale, but I felt that I should have paid him for what I learned in comparing the two versions.

I felt when I started my version that the idea was a short-short; and it should be worth about 1300 words. It was one of those "naturals" that come to a writer now and then, and I wrote it straight through at one sitting. It ran to 2700 words. And it was exactly the way I wanted it. "Cut" said my agent, Mr. Lenniger. So I tried. I really and truly tried. But that was one of the stories I fell in love with, and I simply couldn't leave out a word.

A professional writer friend took the plot almost exactly as it stood and wrote it in about 1500 words. And the emotional impact of the story was tripled. I had used two backgrounds-in a short-short. He used one and brought in the rest of the information in a flashback. The only other major change he made was in the ending. I left the main character worrying about one of her misdeeds. He had her make a sacrifice to set her misdeed right. This main character was a little girl, and I think my friends would agree that in real life my ending would have been true to what a little girl would do; but his story ending was correct of course. I could fairly see the nice old ladies who read it dab at their eyes and say "Poor child. Wasn't she sweet?"

I have a passionate admiration for this professional ability to whittle a story down to its essentials, making every word-yes, every comma-add to the single story effect. Nowhere, I find, is there a wider gulf between my knowing and my doing. Working to overcome this weakness of handling, I read a short story of the type I write, reading it rapidly and at one sitting. I then go straight to the typewriter and write the story from memory. Then I compare the two, to discover where mine is different. Finally I copy the published story word for word. This gives me the feel of how it ought to be written. I know a teacher of [handicapped] children who teaches them to make numerals and letters by writing these on a sheet of paper and then requiring the children to trace the figures over and over until they have the very feel of them in their hands. Copying published stories does that for me.

Second. Curiosity. This is especially helpful in mastering motivation and in getting story ideas. I am forever asking myself, why did Soandso do that? This is especially revealing when a general course of action is considered, rather than what may be merely an impulsive act. I know an executive who is forever trying to sabotage the efforts of any really capable assistant assigned to help him, although he does it under the guise of having unbounded confidence in the assistant. Why? Jealousy? Why is he jealous? Is he aware of what he is doing, or is it subconscious? I know a really brilliant woman chemist who is married to a stupid, careless, unattractive man. Why did she marry him? And why does she continue to stay with him, apparently content?

Equally helpful is my "what-if" curiosity. What if Bill Jones, who has breezed through life with a minimum of trouble because he has that indefinable knack of making everyone love him, were thrust into a situation where he was resented and suspected because of his friendly ways? What if a girl who has a morbid fear of crowds, due to some incident in her past, falls in love with a man who is an idol in the entertainment world? I used that one in a love story which was a pretty good story despite poor handling, and was one of the few I have sold. Put people into impossible situations, work 'em out, and plot will never worry you.

Third. Practice. Stories are made up of different parts-openings, dialogue, high emotional scenes, etc. Some will come easily for you, others must be fought for. Rung two will have taught you what you need most; or perhaps an honest writer friend can tell you, or your agent-critic. Right now I'm working on conveying emotion. Since the purpose of fiction is to make the reader feel, this would seem to be of importance to every writer.

How do you feel when you are "mad enough to spit' for instance? Some writer friends and I got to discussing this one day and were surprised to learn that we all had quite different physical reactions to anger. One girl said she had a sensation of chill, as if a cold wind was blowing across her shoulders. A man said that the cords in his neck grow painfully taut, so that he has difficulty in breathing. A lovely young, miss said that tears spring to her eyes the instant she gets mad, and that makes her madder-and then she must talk fast before she begins to cry!

I think the most valuable single exercise I have found fits in right here. Every night, just before I retire, I sit down at my typewriter for a few minutes. Mentally reviewing the day, I pick out the incident that made me feel most keenly, and try to write it up in such a way that someone else, reading it, would feel as I did at the moment. No story, no plot; just the reason for the emotion, then a description of the accompanying sensations and reactions, and the final action. Those that bear re-reading a month later go into my files, where they often serve handily, when a story character gets fractious. These bits run all the way from annoyance at a trivial happening to biting anger; from amusement at an adult observation from the lips of my ten-year old, to burning anxiety at sudden illness.

Fourth. Writing. Mastering the technique of each part of a story doesn't mean, I find to my sorrow, that you can sit right down and combine the parts and come out with a good story, any more than being an expert four-sifter and shortening-creamer guarantees a perfect cake. In making a cake or a story, the method of combining the ingredients seems to be of paramount, importance. So the final phase of my own plan for learning is just —writing stories. Whole stories, from plot and characters to final fade-out line. I start each one in a fine burst of loving enthusiasm; this, boys and girls, is IT! I finish it in a tizzy of despair; why, oh why is it so difficult to string words together so that they will say exactly what I want them to say? But fortunately, by the time I write the last line of this story there is always another idea burning holes in the pockets of my mind, and so the one that just fell flat doesn't really matter. This next one, you see, will be something well, something!

Third rung from the bottom. That isn't much on the writer's ladder; for this is no kitchen step-ladder with four rungs and a place to sit down. Seems to me, looking up, that it is more like an extension ladder. By the time you get t what looks like the dizzy top from down here, there will probably be a whole new section of rungs shooting up above you. I hope so!

To get back to the study plan. It has done certain concrete things for me. It has taught me more in months than I had learned in several previous years. It has increased my facility with words. I no longer have to fight myself and my Woodstock; we are instead a team. Most significant of all, I can see improvement in my own work over each four-week period.

Maybe this seems like an awful lot of time to spend on finger exercises. I know one amateur who says he never writes a single word that he doesn't hope and expect to sell. Well, maybe. My plan has one thing to recommend it, however, besides what I can see that it is doing for me: it has worked for others, for it is made up of suggestions from people who are now well up the ladder. And I'm willing to bet that I'll get there faster this way than if I went on banging my head against the wall of rejections. I'll wager, too, that if just half of the semi-pro writers to whom this system makes sense actually try it, this third rung is going to get awfully gosh-darn crowded soon.

But that's all right with me. You see, I've already got one foot on the fourth rung, where most of what I write is good enough to be worth revising!

The exercises mentioned:

1.   Take a story and look at the first couple of paragraphs. Ask: "What is the mood of this story going to be?", "How do I know?", "How much information do I now have concerning the characters, story problem, locale?", "Which words gave me that information?"

2.   Read a story, then try to write it from memory. Compare the two versions.

3.   Copy by typing word for word a story you like.

4.   At the end of the day, review the happening that made you feel an emotion the most keenly. No plot or anything, just the direct reason for the emotion. Then describe your reactions and sensations, and what action you took immediately after.

A Fiction Formula That Helped Me Sell 1,000 Stories

By Lee Floren

This article first appeared in the 1958 Writer's Yearbook. Apparently Lee Floren sold a ton of stories, so his advice should carry some weight. Also, be aware there is an emotional kick-in-the-pants story at the end.

AN APPEALING CHARACTER
Strives Against
GREAT ODDS
To Attain
A WORTHWHILE GOAL

T his sign is stapled on the wall over my old desk. Each time I sit down to write my eyes see it.

The sign is over twenty years old, printed on paper now yellow with age. This formula has helped me sell a thousand short stories and novelettes and one hundred books. I think it should be framed in gold.

I firmly believe that any writer who wants to make a living out of authorship, has to write according to the above formula.

This formula is the foundation of your house of words. Let us analyze it, word by word, starting with the noun *character*, then taking the adjective, *appealing*.

AN APPEALING

CHARACTER

Strives Against

GREAT ODDS

To Attain A

WORTHWHILE

 GOAL

Webster defines character as; "A distinctive personality created by a novelist or dramatist."

I shall tell you how I deliberately and cold-bloodedly created two characters.

I had been selling fiction for a year, having made my first sale in 1939 (a Western story) to Mr. Harry Widmer, who is still an editor. The trend was moving away from Western bang-bang.

To keep in the writing business, the author has to follow the trend, or better yet, start another trend. In keeping with this I created Judge Bates, a character who would not be bang-bang crazy, but instead, motivated by sense and judgment.

I thought of an occupation – a way to make a livelihood, if you please. I carefully listed on two sheets of paper all the possible occupations I could think of that would be followed on the Western rangelands and towns.

My eyes stopped on one word: *judge*. My mind flicked over to crusty old Judge Roy Bean, he of the "no law west of the Pecos" fame. A judge could be made into an appealing character, too. My judge would be an honest judge – a traveling jurist who understood cow-country people and problems. I picked the name Judge Lemanuel Bates. To me "Lemanuel" had a sort of a courtly yet dignified ring.

Across my mind, I moved the physical shapes of men – tall, short, fat, homely, handsome.

They stood on a high stage and looked down at me, creative figures in an imaginary line-up. My eyes traveled over them, resting here, there, comparing, shifting; they finally rested at long last on a rather corpulent man slightly below medium height.

"Step out, you," I told this character.

We talked quite a while – as does an author and his characters – in the day dream secret language of author-character.

I found out that he had been born in the Blue Grass country of Kentucky, the year of 1843. His boyhood was that of a poor boy but an ambitious one. At fourteen, he entered the office of a local barrister, and studied law. Then, the Civil War.

He came out with one minor wound, a major at the age of twenty-two. The South was in turmoil, he had itchy boots, and he trekked to Wyoming, there to hang up his shingle in a little trail town called Cow Trail. Within a year, he was local judge; two more years, a traveling jurist. When Wyoming entered the Union as a Territory, he became the first federal judge.

He was smart, ambitious as I had noticed, and as we talked in our secret language, I saw a savage small-burning flame in him – and that flame was the desire to be just in all decisions. Freud might call it an over compensating thrust for self magnification. In the kind of fiction I was writing, such phrasing has no place; but between character and author there must be a deep full understanding of not only *what* the character is but *why*.

"You're my man," I told him.

So he stepped out then, complete and appealing, into a Western short story, and he carried the story – completely following the above formula – into the pages of *Big Book Western*, then edited, by Mr. Mike Tilden.

Across two decades, Judge Bates and I have had many, many serious talks. He has raised legal and moral points that have sent me stumblingly to local barristers and into books on psychology.

"How do you eye the female world?" I asked.

His answer was straight and from the shoulder, befitting his character. "I have a great eye for a well-turned thigh and a well-filled blouse, Lee. But I don't think I should marry."

"Why not?"

"Let's look at it objectively." (He has a legal-trained mind, this meal ticket of mine.) "My position as a judge requires I move constantly into danger. This would not be fair to any woman who married me." Here his eyes twinkled. "And besides, marriage, to me, is a ball and chain."

I smiled. "You're hired, Judge Bates."

He stopped at my studio door. "How about a partner? I might get lonesome, all by myself and, besides, a story starring two men is always more popular. There can be conflict between two partners."

I nodded. "Let's run the line-up again."

So we did and, on the third run, we found Judge Bates' partner, a bony man, gangling and tall, who always chewed tobacco.

"Your name?"

"Tobacco Jones."

"Tobacco?"

He hocked an oyster into my spittoon. "Good as any, ain't it?"

So... we let it ride, like that. To my surprise, he knew Judge Bates. "I'm postmaster in Cow Trail. Judge Bates got me my job." He couldn't read or write.

Tobacco Jones was a year younger than the judge. Born in Ohio, he had been a private in the Civil War but escaped unwounded. When he heard that Judge Bates had been a colonel for the South and he only a private for the Union, he frowned and bit off another chew of Horseshoe.

"He might try to pull his rank on me," he growled. "Sometimes I think the South won an' didn't lose."

"Has he pulled rank on you yet?"

"Oh, onct or twict."

"Make you mad?"

A Fiction Formula That Helped Me Sell 1,000 Stories

"Hell, I can't get mad at Judge Bates." Tobacco Jones unlimbered to his gaunt height. "He cain't get hot at me, either."

"How about females?"

"From a distance, Lee. A great distance."

"You got the job," I told him.

So with short Judge Lemanuel Bates rode the gaunt, scowling, Tobacco Jones. Together they have ridden their way into the memories of persons all over this globe – black people, white, Orientals. They are known from the Arctic to the Antarctic. Their adventures have been translated into many foreign tongues.

I gave them hates, fears, terror, love and all the other emotions mankind is capable of feeling always digging into their past for convincing motivations.

Let's get to the adjective, *appealing*.

What makes a character – a fictitious person – appealing to the readers? Why do you, as an individual, like some persons – and dislike others?

Only a trained person working in the wide field of human relationships – a psycho-analyst, or some person trained by long study and practice in the field of human relationships – could answer that question adequately.

Many of the letters I receive from readers leave the impression that they are sure Judge Bates once lived– a real live flesh and blood Wyoming jurist.

I believe that can be explained thusly: I tried to make him human.

He was so real *in my mind* that through the typewritten page I made him actual and real in the minds of my readers. I believe I know his character better than I know my own.

In one sense, this is logical; I created him, he did not create me.

I tried to give him the breath of man, the appetites of man, the thousands of other emotions that conflict within the breast of mankind.

Anthropologists say we are at one and the same time the imitative, cunning playful monkey, the hungry, selfish savage and the civilized cultivated man of affairs. All three of these – the monkey, the savage and the civilized man must make peace within our mind at the same time. That's where the trouble comes in. None of us are divorced from our heritage. For a character to be

13

real, he shares this same heritage with all of mankind.

Judge Bates to me has more than mere physical properties – height, weight, color of hair and eyes. What he does and says comes not out of my environment and heredity; these spring from *his* past, *his* inheritance.

Sometimes he takes over his own story. He scans the written page and says, "Lee, that scene is not written correctly."

"What do you mean?" On guard.

"I am a peaceful man. I don't fight unless in defense of my person or my principles. In that scene you have me deliberately provoking fisticuffs."

He is right, but I am loathe to admit it because the scene is done and has some phrasing that delights me.

"That scene is not in line with my character. Besides, people will not like me if I – a judge – a man of trust – deliberately provoke a fight. Rewrite it, please?"

Judge Bates wants people to like him. Almost all humans possess this trait. Therefore Judge Bates is again proving he is a human.

I sit in sullen silence momentarily, then tear the paper from my machine. (He always seems to come out victor.) He says nothing but, back of his eyes, there is a twinkle. For now he is, in one sense, the creator; I am a mere interpreter.

This man I have created – this man who is merely a product of my imagination – is, at these moments, stronger than I, and I marvel at the greatness of creative effort.

I rewrite the scene. He nods. "That scene is now in character," he compliments me.

N one of us can dictate to the other how he should I write his story. We can attempt to teach him how to write his story but beyond that we cannot go. For there burns in each of us who wants to write a flame and the flame's name is Creation, and in creation lies Strife.

Let us look at this verb, *strives*.

Logic proclaims two types of strife: physical and mental. The action story (Western, detective, air war, sports, etc.) is concerned mainly with physical action, physical strife – snarling guns, roaring hoofs, tires squealing on blacktop. Yet a competent writer can weave into the action story the threads of mental struggle.

This gives the story conviction. Characters are more appealing when linked closer to human reality.

I shall have to dig into my own writing past as an author to emphasize what I consider the difference between mental and physical strife. For years I pounded out action material – Westerns, detectives, air-war, sports stories – and when the all-fiction pulps collapsed, I turned to writing love books.

I have written five. All have sold as hardcovers.

To keep one's work in print, one has to be adaptable; my change-over was not easy, I can assure you, and many of the globules, I am sure, were not composed of sweat – they were blood.

I had to switch from a field where physical action was foremost with mental strife secondary to a field where all decisions, all plot, depended, almost solely, on mental turmoil.

Recently I wrote on order for Miss Lucy Mabry, editor at Thomas Bourgey Co., what Miss Mabry calls "the career love story." With this type of story, one deals in two fields – entertainment and education. The entertainment feature is involvement in the love element; the educational, in showing the reader how one works – the tasks involved – in a particular career.

Miss Mabry and I selected, after some correspondence, a heroine caught in the throes of fearing she loved two men, not just one. Her goal, then, was to find happiness – to determine which man she loved the more. Making this choice involved the angle of mental indecision.

The other part of the novel – always secondary to the love struggle – is designed to show the reader, most of whom are young girls and young women, the workings of some particular trade or profession.

In this particular book, we decided to illustrate for the reader the workings of a Hollywood trade newspaper – a sheet filled with gossip about TV and movie personalities in the entertainment field.

These conclusions laboriously reached, we then settled upon our choice of heroine, who, in this case, had to be a reporter or editor for this newspaper. I wrote the first ten pages and a brief synopsis and Miss Mabry mailed me a contract and an advance.

Our story had a combination of mental indecision and physical action. The mental indecision, of course, wavered between the choice of this man or that, as a husband. The physical action involved the editing of the heroine's column, the intra-office politics and strife, the actual mechanical processes employed in getting the newspaper out on the street.

We deliberately picked Hollywood as the setting, for Hollywood to the average reader spells glamour and romance.

So, I wrote the book.

That sounds easy, doesn't it? So, I wrote the book! Five words, nothing more. But how much more there was than those five words! ...

First I established the characters completely and convincingly in my mind. What were the backgrounds of these characters involved? I made them real humans – humans of flesh and blood and desire and emotional – or else I could not transmit them.

Were I to fail in this transmission, I would have failed in my obligations as an author. I would have violated my duties to my editor and my readers. And, from another angle, this violation of trust would have kept the story from print.

Carefully, from a telephone book, I selected surnames for my characters, making sure I had no two surnames starting with the same letter for, Stratton and Stanton, both in the same story, add to reader's confusion. This accomplished, I then gave them given names, also by skipping around the telephone book, making sure no given names started with the same letter.

Then, laboriously, I built backgrounds for my characters, writing down among other things the temperaments of their homes, their educations, their childhoods, their hates, fears, loves, desires. For each character I wrote a page of past history – thereby establishing the person, complete with moods and flesh-and-blood, in my mind.

What was the goal of each character? No goal, no purpose; no purpose, no story. One played all angles, cutting whatever throat necessary, to succeed in his profession.

Another was cagey, playing cards close, working and scheming, to reach his goal. And this one blundered, letting heads fall, to reach his destination.

Each has his goal in life established. Each became a complete well-rounded character in my mind. My job, then, is to transfer them to paper, so millions can enjoy their strife, their desires, their hopes and fears.

Because, if they have human attributes, they will be interesting to the reader, because the reader is a part of humanity, and he wants to identify himself with the whole of humanity.

Which brings us to the section of the formula. I believe there are two types of goals toward which humanity strives. One is the high and hard to attain goal of spiritual tranquility toward which all humanity, now seemingly more than at any time in human history, is seeking to reach.

The other goal consists of material things.

The action story (such as a Western) is more concerned with material goals than is the slick-paper (or quality) story.

Thousands of Westerns have been written concerning the struggle for water, for grazing land, for mining claims. Undoubtedly, thousands more will someday be published, their characters fighting, dying, laughing, drunk and sober, and these thousands of unwritten stories will concern the goals mentioned.

Let us consider briefly one of these elements: water.

Water in the semi-arid – and arid – West was, literally life itself. Characters controlling water controlled, indirectly, all the humans in that area.

Let's say we have a character selected, complete in our minds, and he is a homesteader, seeking only to find peace in hard work. Because he came into the land early, he had a chance to homestead a major water-hole, which he did — thereby taking its use away from a powerful cattle-king.

And the cattle-king fights to get it back.

The homesteader is an appealing character, for he represents, indirectly, the masses of humanity – the people desiring only peace, a home and a chance to work at what they like.

Naturally he has the sympathy of the reader. Because he has that sympathy, he possesses the reader's interest. But to hold it, the author has to make the homesteader's goal – this keeping possession of his land and water – vital and extremely necessary. When the goal is thin, so is the reader interest. We shall add, then, a wife and three toddlers. This increases the value of his goal. It also adds mental strife to his character.

This cattle-king is ruthless. He has ruled this land for two decades like a feudal lord, holding his reign through fear. What if I am killed, thinks the homesteader? What, then, of my wife and my three children?

The cattle-king's objective is to get him off the water-hole. How the cattle-king does this depends upon the tenets of his character. If ruthless, he rides with gunmen, sheer and brutal power on horseback.

If a schemer, he will resort to legal methods.

So each character, in his own way, builds the story's plot, letting the writer merely translate his actions and thoughts. Each word uttered, each action – overt or otherwise, comes out of the value of the goal, out of the character of the individuals involved.

Then, when the goal is reached – when one has lost and the other has won – the story is over.

Now to the spiritual goals.

We shall say, for example, a young man wants to help humanity, better the lot of his fellow-man, to find in his work a tranquility of soul, a purpose to his life.

Many intangible foes could face him. Perhaps he is poor and needs money for religious training. To make that element more dangerous to his goal, perhaps he, too, is married and has a family to support. Thus, we have increased his struggle, put a hurdle between the character and his goal.

Other impediments can be added. (A successful story is the tale of an appealing character surmounting great odds for a worthwhile goal.) His wife perhaps has not complete faith in him and in herself, for a minister's wife carries heavy responsibilities.

Some thinking can stir to life other impediments.

How he surmounts these impediments, be they social or physical, constitutes the plot of our story.

Every word – yes, every word – in a story is of definite purpose, and that purpose is either to advance the plot or characterize characters. If it has neither of these purposes, then it has no place in your story. Either you, the author, pencil it out, or the editor shall. Descriptive passages are useful only to the extent that they give reality to the plot or help explain a character's action.

All stories are hard to write for all authors. There is in each story a point where the author falters, caught in his own step, stands in stony silence in thought, then goes ahead in his best manner, wondering at his inadequateness.

I am never satisfied with any of my stories or books. When the day comes that I finish a story and say to myself, "It is perfect," then on that minute, that day, that year, I am through forever as an author.

I know that day will never come.

Many times I am asked by would-be authors, "Where do you get your ideas?"

We live in a beautiful world of greenery and golden sunshine. Around us are millions of people – laughing, fighting, struggling, smiling through glistening teeth – and a world that essentially is good and only perverted by a few ambitious, deadly individuals.

These people marry, beget, rear children. They love and hate, they create and destroy, they sometimes kill by love and sometimes by outright murder. Nobody knows much about them, and they know less about themselves.

Some live in roiling cities, some live on green slopes, some live on water, some in the air, some in dark holes called mines. But essentially, basically, they all have one combining desire – the desire to find happiness, an integration of their own talents and surroundings. This sense of happiness might assume different forms for each individual, but the drive is inside nonetheless.

How then can one ask, "Where do you get your ideas?" You get them from everyday living – a child coming into your studio and putting his arms around you, tender and thoughtful and very wise; the bark of a dog on the lawn in black night; the proud arch of the sun over glistening Mount San Jacinto.

One has to be blind – mentally and spiritually – not to see he is surrounded by ideas for stories.

Let me tell you a little story.

In 1946 I met an admirable character. We met in an odd place – the Animal Shelter in Santa Barbara. She was in a cage – golden brown with slashes of glistening white – and she leaped happily when she saw me.

So Miss Letye Jones moved into my home – and my heart.

Born on the island that gave her her name, she came to the U.S., an orphan. Together she and I walked the green rolling foothills of Old Mexico. We fished the roaring Two Medicine, we hunted quail in the Sierra Juarez. She nipped the cows on the heels in Iowa.

I watched the cataracts grow slowly. Last Thanksgiving Eve she stumbled to my chair, sat down, as if to say, "This is it." For two hours an eye specialist – an M. D. – worked. I watched his skilled hands, delicate yet so strong and sure; I saw the eyes peeled open, the grisly cataracts lifted.

I saw the anesthetic hypoed into the vein of her leg. I saw her slip into a dark sleep she did not understand. I saw the rise and fall of her ribs as she sucked in life-giving oxygen.

And I saw her raise her bloody head, after the cone was removed, when I said, "Hi, Letye," and I saw her look vainly for the owner of the voice she had known for twelve years.

She never saw again.

She died a few days ago.

She died not from the operation. She died from the savage loneliness of the dark that she could not understand or comprehend.

Why am I telling you this?

Because I stood there, and I watched, one side of me held pity and fear, but on the other side was working the cold analytical mind of an author. Each movement of that surgeon's skilled fingers etched in my brain. The grind of a movie camera recording the operation for the veterinarians, the damp sweat on the surgeon's forehead—all these I remember. And out of this came the germ, the plot idea, for two books.

One shall be a light-love book, a girl training to be a veterinarian, fighting against the restrictions of her sex in that field. Her goal will be to overcome those man-made restrictions, assert the efficiency of her sex, and attain the happiness she desires.

And the other will be a story of Leyte, and the title is already in my mind, the plot in sketchy form, and the title shall be Her Name Was Leyte.

Where do you get your ideas?

The next time a would-be author asks that question of me I shall not answer.

He was never meant to be an author.

Again, here is the formula:

AN APPEALING CHARACTER
Strives Against
GREAT ODDS
To Attain
A WORTHWHILE GOAL

One of my favorite lines here is this: "What was the goal of each character? No goal, no purpose; no purpose, no story." Keeping the character's goal in mind helps keep the story on track. It helps keep the reader involved.

A Very Simple System

by William Benton Johnston

This article comes from the October, 1940 issue of Writer's Digest. The short version is this: Always send out/publish the very best fiction you are capable of producing. No phoning it in.

I would rather sell a good story to *Grit* for five dollars than a bad one to *Collier's* for five hundred dollars.

Screwy? In view of the fact that I am a professional writer-and plan to continue in this business-I think not. The good story would advance me toward my ultimate goal; the bad one would take me back a step. Against this, four hundred and ninety-five dollars loses significance. I'm no long-haired artist. I'm almost bald and an a hardworking "money writer".

In the beginning, I evolved a very simple plan: to select a plot and write a story I around it, *putting into every paragraph the very best of my ability.*

You'll probably say: "I've read some of your stuff that was awful tripe."

True enough, but it was my best at the time and I have no apologies for it; only regrets.

After eight years and some two hundred and Seventy-five published stories-and read hundreds of theories–I'm using that same system. Perhaps it is because I am too dumb to learn a better method, or because the old one has supported me, and my family, all those years.

Some beginner, confused by so much varied and often complicated advice, may find the simplicity of this one-rule system a steadying influence.

Using it, I do not write a pulp or a slick yarn; I write a story and do my damnedest to make it good. This may seem artless and unorthodox, but here are some actual results:

(a) A short-short, written with a one cent market in mind, sold for forty cents per word.

(b) A western, intended for the pulps, landed me in one of the big weeklies, to which I have made three subsequent sales.

I n 1933, I was doing a few yarns for *All-America Sports,* at twelve to fifteen dollars per story. I had such a script in my pocket, ready for mailing, one day when I met Henry G. Rhodes on the streets of Memphis. He read the story and suggested that I try a thirty-five cents slick with it. The yarn was bought and featured; since then I have sold that publication thousands of dollars worth of fiction, with only one rejection.

Doesn't going over each story, putting everything you have into it, cut down on production? Yes, it does. My agent sometimes calls me on the carpet about this, but in other letters, he says:

(a) "Enclosed herewith is my check for the story which we sold to [X] last week. The story wasn't so wonderful; the plot material was trite indeed, yet I must admit that excellent writing and careful characterization put it across..."

(b) "We felt all along that this one, despite the fact that you really dovetailed two stories into one, would sell, for it had the virtues of being beautifully written and of presenting real living human beings."

I n trying to prove that constant efforts at perfection pays, this article may seem, a personal success story. Nothing could be farther from truth. I'm nowhere near the top and I may never get any closer. I mentioned that my writing has supported a family for eight years. Supported, in this instance, is a flexible word. Sometimes the going was pretty tough, and the meals anything but pretty. The family's attitude has been swell, taking the cornbread and peas along with the caviar-and no grumbling.

For the past eight years and a half, it hasn't been so bad, because I have been fortunate in having the assistance of an agent with a keen story sense and a broad knowledge of markets. So now I just write the yarns and he sees that my efforts are shown to the proper books. Even the dog, Amos, is getting fat.

All this in defense of my simple system. Now let's see how it works-in practice.

Several years ago, I was writing a serial and having a hard time with the plot (long fiction has always been my nemesis). The finished story was far from satisfactory. In fact, the whole thing was so hopeless that I grumbled about the long and tedious work of rewriting it paragraph by paragraph, cutting out every word that I could and re-casting clumsy sentences.

A writer friend of mine said: "Send it out a time or two 'as is'-maybe you'll get a nibble."

It was a temptation. That kind of re-write on a serial adds up to work. Yet I decided that anything was better than making too bad an impression on editors. It took a couple of weeks to go over the manuscript and polish it up.

Mark Mellen was editor of *Post Time.* I sent the story there. In due time, came a letter:

"Your *'Valkyre of Cumberland Hall'* received and first installment has gone forward to illustrator...

"I had another serial on my desk, with perhaps a better plot, but *not so well written* as yours..."

I have that original script in my desk, together with the revised version. Let's look at the changes. Not particular good writing in either instance, but the difference between a rejection and a substantial check.

(a) **Original.**

The sale of stock to Cumberland Hall was successful so far as attendance went and when it was over, the old shedrow was empty save far the one occupied by Tallahatchie.

After the crowd had drift£ed away, Betty and Allen sat in the office. Allen's face was clouded with worry.

"The auctioneer did his best," he admitted "and we sold them all, still we lack $2,400 and the note is due tomorrow."

Betty looked at her bank book.

"We have $1,900 here, Allen."

"You need that for current expenses."

"We'll live on bread and water. Mr. Gray must be paid in full. For some reason he wants Cumberland Hall- and badly."

Allen figured again. "All of which comes to-five hundred short."

"You can cipher up the darndest things." Betty laughed. "Here, take this, jump in your roadster, drive down to Nashville and sell it." She slipped a diamond ring from her finger and passed it across the desk.

"But, Betts, that was your graduation present."

"Never mind; Gray must be paid."

Allen drove away and, in the late afternoon, hitch-hiked his way back to Cumberland Hall.

"Where is your car?" Betty asked when he walked up the graveled drive.

"A crazy guy in Benjestown offered me six hundred and fifty bucks for it. Imagine a goof that screwy!"

He took the ring from his pocket and tossed it to her.

"Here's your glassware; we won't need it now."

With a little cry, Betty ran down and flung herself into his arms.

"That car was the only valuable possession you had left. Allen, you should done it."

She pushed him away and looked at him. "If I lost Cumberland Hall and everything else I have in the world, I'd be rich having you, Allen Lamar."

(a) Revised Copy.

When the stock sale was over, Tallahatchie was all that was left of Cumberland Hall stables.

"The auctioneer did his best, Allen admitted to Betty,"and yet we're five hundred short."

She slipped a diamond ring off her finger and gave it to him. Take this to Nashville and sell it.

"But, Betts-"

She said it again, "Take it to Nashville and sell it."

Allen returned in late afternoon, walking. "A guy in Benjestown bought my car," he explained.

"Imagine, six hundred bucks for that old wreck!" He gave Betty back her ring. "We don't need to sell it now."

For a moment she stood there and stared at him, then came down the steps very slowly and put her arms around him.

"If I lose Cumberland Hall and everything else that I possess," she said gently, "I'll always be rich–as long as I have you."

(b) Original.

Jed Huskins came around the beech tree and shook hands

with Jurden.

"What you want with me?"

"I got a job for you." Jurden told him.

"What is it?" Jurden took out a wallet and counted from it a hundred dollars. "Sometime this morning, Jed, a horse van from Cumberland Hall Stables is going to leave Benjestown for Louisville. Now, that van will have a big black horse with a white star in his face, aboard. I don't want that horse to go a bit farther than these hills; I want him taken from the van and killed, see?"

Jed Huskins thoughtfully took a chew of home-made twist tobacco.

"That van will have to come close to here; it'll have to come right along Durveen Pike, the loneliest stretch of road in this country."

"Exactly." Jurden grinned evilly. "It ought not to be much trouble."

Huskins reached out and took the money.

"It won't be no trouble a-tall," he drawled.

(b) Revised Copy.

Jed Huskins came around the beech tree.

Jurden said, "Jed, I've got a job for you."

"What is it?"

Jurden opened his wallet and counted out a hundred dollars. "Sometime this morning, a Cumberland Hall van is leaving Benjestown for Louisville; a black horse with a star in his face will be aboard. I want that horse removed from the van and destroyed."

Jed Huskins took out a plug of tobacco and bit off a chew. "The van will come along Durveen Pike, the lonsomest stretch of road in this here country."

Jurden grinned. "Exactly-it ought not to be much trouble."

Jed reached out and took the hundred dollars.

"No trouble a-tall," he said.

L et me try to prove, in another way, that I write without the handicap of slants, pulp or slick. The opening paragraphs quoted below are from four of my stories: two pulps and two slicks. Can you denote any particular difference?

(1)   The house was new and unmellowed, and the cleared ground around it made a brown scar on the green, far-

reaching length of the valley. Yet there was already a home-like atmosphere here, manifest in bright curtains and planted flowers and consideration of small details which showed a woman's care and pride.

I t was a pretty place, too, with the up-sweep of the hills back of it and, beyond these, stony summits making their high, irregular pattern against the sky. Before it, the mesa ran into the far distance, smooth and flat and unbroken. ("*Homesteader,*" *Dime Western,* Feb., 1940.)

(2)   Mrs. Molly Brown's cottage stood on the outskirts of the little town of Barclay. It was a neat place, with orderly hedges and close-cropped lawn. In the rear, there were clean, well-arranged chicken runs and row after row of apple trees. Just outside the front gate, a sign announced that apples, fresh yard eggs and blooded Minorcas and Plymouth Rocks were for sale. ("*The Eye of Death,*" *Secret Agent X,* Feb., 1938.)

(3)   White thunderheads lay like puffs of carnival taffy against the blue dome of the China sky. Wayne Driscoll, with a veteran's instinct for advantage, lurked in the blindspot of the sun and throttled the Curtiss combat ship to idling speed. The deadly little plane fretted as a high-strung thoroughbred fret under heavy, restraining wraps.

W ayne chuckled: a hell of a place to be thinking of horses. Seven thousand feet above the broad Yangtze, with Nanking sprawled like a helpless giant before the Japanese bombers coming over Pootung from their carriers anchored at the mouth of the Whangpoo.

Yet the human mind sometimes becomes strangely detached during crucial moments, groping into the past as if attempting to fix clearly old, familiar scenes against the endless stretch of eternity. ("*No More Guns,*" *Turf and Sports Digest,* June, 1939.)

(4)   There was an unrealness about the entire scene, as if someone had splashed gay colors against a grim and sombre canvas.

First, the flowers blooming in the arid soil beside the walls of the old Territory prison. Then the little girl, with her deep blue eyes and bright print dress, leaning against those drab, tragedy-enclosing walls, laughing at something the Maricopa said as he lugged water up from the Colorado and filled a barrel at the garden's edge. Then, too, the mere fact that the Kid was there, carrying water for flowers and making a little girl laugh and follow his movements with adoring eyes. (*"A Well Remembered Kiss,"* *Liberty,* June, 1940.)

I remember reading an article by a "million-words-a-year man" in which he ridiculed the idea of going over and rewriting pulp material. He said, in effect, "Rewriting or revising cent-a-word stuff is equivalent to getting half a cent for it—slave wages. Better to hammer it out, charge off your rejections and let volume take care of you."

I watched the progress of this man for quite a time. I've forgotten his name, but he was contemporary of H. Bedford-Jones, Ernest Haycox and Cleve Adams. The conclusion is obvious, isn't it?

I know the old gag about "An amateur writes a story and looks for a market; a professional looks at a market and writes a story."

Naturally I "study markets"; a thing which every writer must do. But it doesn't mean to study a small, fourth-rate one and then decide that you can meet its requirements without putting forth your best effort.

You are not writing for that particular magazine; you're writing a story with your name signed to it. You're laying a stone in the foundation upon which you hope to build a stairway to *Liberty* or *Collier's* or *The Saturday Evening Post.*

You are advertising yourself as a good or a poor writer. Every story is a vote one way or the other.

I liked this one because it's advice is contrary to some that your read elsewhere- it's something to at least think about. Writing really fast is great, but not necessary. Perhaps slowing down a bit isn't the worst idea.

The Requisites for Success

By Bill Rendered

From the June 1920 issue of Writer's Monthly.

A bout regularly once a month, someone tells me, rather wistfully, that he is pretty sure he could write stories, but that he has no spare time.

I always like to hear this because it is so human. No one in this, the present year of our Lord, 1920, has any spare time. If you told a society woman who spent three hours a day having her nails manicured that she had spare time, she would pierce you with a look through a lorgnette that would cripple you for life. Having her nails pruned and cultivated is just part of her routine, for the evening's exhibition. If you told a farmer who sits behind the kitchen stove all winter that he had spare time, he would run you through with a hoe handle, because he is just planning for next season. If you told a business man who leaves the office at 11.30 a. m. and returns from dinner at 2.30 p. m. that he had spare time, he would brain you with a planked steak, and then smother you with onions. He is just taking that necessary food and rest which stimulates him to greater endeavor!

Thomas, Richard and Harold, April, May and June, work in offices or somewhere else. Monday night they go to the movies; Tuesday night they play bridge; Wednesday night they read; Thursday night they have a talk-fest about folks they know; Friday night they go to the movies again; Saturday night they have a party, and Sunday they take it easy, being too tired to go to church. It is all a part of the routine, however. They are doing it to fit them for the grind of the office. They have no spare time whatever. For this reason none could make the attempt at story writing, no matter how great was the desire–no spare time, you see!

Set this down in your notebook with a little indelible pencil: Anyone who really wants to try to write stories that will sell will do it, and seventeen yoke of oxen and nineteen bulls can't stop them.

Over in Fall River, the city of tall chimneys, they have a slogan which reads: "Fall River Looms Up. That's just what writing does to those who think they want to try it. It "looms up" as something big and difficult, to be tackled some time when there is a whole lot of "spare time, but a great many who think they would like to try the game never do it because the "spare time," in their conception of the thing, never comes! These people did not really want to write. They only thought they did.

The very least of the attributes required for those who want to write stories that the editors will buy is "spare time." The most essential thing required is the desire to write *above all other things,* and to have the interest, enthusiasm and vim for it that will not allow defeat. To the one thus armed, rejection slips serve only as a stimulant to overcome them. In all this world there is no greater stimulant to one who knows no defeat than opposition. It increases the desire ten-fold to do that which you intend to do.

Did not one of the greatest women writers of today write her first story "amid a multitude of household duties?" Did not one of our greatest writers of Western tales write his first story in a saw mill, "with one eye on a two-foot buzz-saw to see that it didn't cut off the hand that held the pencil?" Did not one of our greatest novelists write a best-seller during a summer's vacation that he took to get rested? The early struggles of seven-tenths of the big writers of today, as told by themselves and their friends, show that they wrote under all sorts of handicaps and under all sorts of adverse and unfavorable conditions. But they *wanted to write,* and opposition was powerless before them.

If you really want to write, *more than anything else,* you'll find the "spare time to do it. But you must have the enthusiasm and vim, and you must have them to the extent of overcoming obstacles-rejection slips–discouragements–perhaps the sentiments of your acquaintances that you can't do it. But if you have the great attributes required, you'll win! And I surely hope that you do, for to those who love it writing is the most fascinating work in the whole wide world.

THE REQUISITES FOR SUCCESS

I find it hilarious that nobody has ever felt that they had any free time just lying around. Even in the 1920's they thought life was too busy.

Also, I wonder who the saw-mill author is.

31

BREATH OF LIFE

by Marian B. Cockrell

From Writer's Digest, August, 1943.

N o one thing in writing fiction is so important that nothing else matters, but I think that making the characters in stories individuals who are real and believable, instead of male and female puppets moved about by the author arbitrarily for the purposes of his plot with no consideration for their feelings (and how can one consider their feelings if he doesn't know what they are?) is so important that it is impossible to write a good story without it.

It is said that there are no new plots. But there are new people. No person in the world is exactly like another, and no character in a story, presented by a writer who knows him well, is exactly like any other that was ever depicted by anyone else. Even such fundamentally exciting things as violence and death are interesting in fiction only according to whom they happen to. If the reader doesn't care whether a character lives or dies, then whether he does or not is completely unimportant.

If there is a man on a submarine who likes to be on submarines, then the fact that he is on one is not very interesting in itself, and the reader waits impatiently for something to happen that will arouse his Interest. But if the man on the submarine suffers from claustrophobia, why the mere fact that he is there, before any action whatever takes place, produces the sense of anticipation in the reader that is so important in persuading him to finish the story.

A plot has to be credible and interesting. Its basis may be quite fantastic, but the story is made perfectly credible if the people engaged in the action are the kind of people who would act that way. Or the plot may be about things intrinsically dull and Commonplace, but made absorbing by the kind of people these dull things are happening to.

I read an article in the *Writer's Year Book* called "*Tag Your Characters*" and the general idea was to be sure and give each character some individual idiosyncrasy, such as a habit of biting his nails, or always remembering names, or never getting a haircut, so that the reader could always tell them apart. I think that is a step in the right direction, but to my mind arbitrary tagging merely for purposes of identification is sliding lazily over the most important thing in the story. The reader should be able to tell the characters apart with ease, without the device of having different colored ribbons around their necks. Of course, people do have idiosyncrasies, and the ones the people in the story have should be included, but they should spring from the personality of the character, and the writer should know very definitely what that is.

I have written a good many short stories, and have sold about a third of them. I searched for interesting, unusual plots (none of them were, very) and some of the stories sold and some didn't. They were all written with the same care and in much the same style. On looking them over and analyzing the plots, I have come to the conclusion that if synopses were made of them all, of the bare fiction, no one on earth could possibly tell which were the ones that sold and which weren't. But on reading the stories the difference is immediately apparent. The ones which sold were stories about real, living people (I don't mean portraits from life) who aroused the reader's interest and anticipation before they had *done* anything at all.

And a character doesn't have to be particularly unusual to be the kind of person people like to read about. He simply has to be alive. He can be the village idiot and have the reader palpitating with anxiety because he can't find his other shoe, if the reader knows what it means to him to find it. The reader has to know him as a person-not a type, not a shadowy shape.

I don't mean that one should go into tedious detail about the life and appearance and psychology of every character in his story. There isn't time, and it slows up action. But the writer should know so much about his character that he can indicate his personality and emotions with very few words.

Suppose one decides to write a story about Joe, a typical high

33

school boy. He will do this and this. So it is written, and it was supposed to be funny, or tragic, but somehow it doesn't quite come off. So-suppose we start over.

What is a typical high school boy? And of course the answer to that is, there isn't any. Well, what is this particular boy, who happens to be going to high school, like? The practical thing to do is write a short biography, a character sketch. What kind of people are his parents, how much money have they, what kind of home, what does Joe think of them, what kind of girls does he like, who are his friends, how does he stand in school, what are his interests?

By the time the writer has done a page or so about Joe, probably completely extemporaneous, he knows things about him that never occurred to him when he was writing the story the first time. And when he writes it over he may suddenly say to himself, "But Joe wouldn't do that. He wouldn't feel that way about it at all. And if this happens to him, what difference does it make? He doesn't care. Let that happen to him instead. That would be terribly important to Joe." And that is the time when he changes his plot, and when he *doesn't* try to jam Joe into the one he had originally, because Joe wouldn't be comfortable there.

The writer knows Joe so well by now that the reader knows him too, and if Joe is made to act or react unnaturally the reader will resent it. And there are things in the story about Joe that reveal his personality, things the writer couldn't have put in the first time, because he didn't know them himself.

If the writer is absolutely determined to use the original plot, why he must change Joe's name (because by now he knows Joe too well-he'll have to write it about someone else) and invent a boy who *would* do those things, and feel them; and then he'll write with conviction and the reader will feel what he feels.

In writing a book, of course, convincing characters are even more important than in a short story, and one should be especially thorough in getting acquainted with his people before he starts writing. Even then they will grow and develop and sometimes run away with the plot entirely. And a plot that has been run away with is usually a good plot, for the people in it have had enough vigor in them to insist on being themselves.

These things apply to any kind of story. It is perfectly possible to lay down a detective story with a yawn in the midst of spouting blood and sudden death. I have read a great many detective and mystery stories where the sole interest of the reader could only be the mental problem of who done-it-and a few where the characters were so interesting to read about that the book would have been good whether anybody ever got murdered or not. And these are the best ones, and the most successful. They are interesting novels.

In writing any kind of story it is important to remember that in fiction *nothing* is important except in relation to the people it happens to. *Anything* can be important if it happens to, or is done by, the right person. If a writer has a character, or characters, who are interesting and unusual personalities, they can go through the most commonplace actions and incidents, and hold the reader's interest completely. Or an unusual or exciting plot can be written about the most ordinary run-of-the-mill people, and if they are real and alive they can produce an absorbing story merely by their reactions to an unusual situation.

Having written the paragraph above, it occurs to me that of the two books I have written, the first was about ordinary people faced with an unusual situation, and the second was about an unusual girl's reactions to the most everyday experiences possible.

A friend of mine, who has read innumerable books on writing, read the second book in manuscript form, and told me when she had finished, that if she didn't know already that the book had been sold, she could tell me dozens of things that were wrong with it.

"The fact that it's sold doesn't mean that it's perfect," I said. "But did you find it interesting to read?"

"Oh yes," she said. "I was so afraid that girl was going to marry Martin. But I think you should have more in it about Giles."

"But he's just a sub-character, and the rules you've been talking about-"

"I don't care about the rules. I liked him. I want to know more about him."

"There you are. There *are* dozens of things wrong with it. It would be a better book if there weren't. I've written only two books and don't know as much about novel construction as I should. But the characters are alive and make you interested in them, and anxious to see what happens to them, and the book is going to be published because of that, and in spite of the dozens of things that are wrong with it. And if the construction were perfect and the characters dead it wouldn't have been. Maybe next time I can get them both right, but the people in it are the part that has to be right no matter what. (I did put in more about Giles, because I had got interested in him too).

Successful fiction is fiction that is interesting to read, in which the people behave consistently and don't let the reader down; and one may follow every rule of construction in all the books and still come up with something anyone would go to sleep over. Or one may write a story which contains flagrant violations of some of the rules of the how-to-write boys, and still know that it is right and the way it ought to be, and someone will buy it while his drawn-with-a-ruler stories are still making the weary rounds.

I don't mean that one should ignore the sensible and helpful rules that are generally acknowledged to be good. But if a writer finds he can't use them in a particular instance, he shouldn't let them get in his hair.

If a writer with any ability to express himself knows his characters and presents them faithfully without trying to twist them out of shape to suit *him*, and has them do and experience things that are important to *them*, he has accomplished the most important thing in fiction writing. All the other things one has to learn are important too, but not *that* important.

I had the thought while reading this that contrast makes characters interesting. Exaggeration makes them interesting. A mundane person reacting to an extreme situation is interesting as well as a larger-than-life character in a mundane situation (think Mr. Incredible as an insurance functionary.)

Marian also mentions tags, which are now a common concept in fiction writing. And I believe what she may have have been getting at it what we now call traits. Tags being specific descriptive words that are only used with one character, and traits being actions and attitudes that one character embodies. Both are useful for creating a memorable impression of a character in the mind of a reader.

Butch and His Big Ears

By Fannie Hurst

This article was originally published in the April 1946 issue of Writer's Digest.

W hat is it that has neither taste, form, nor color? Editors cry for it. Authors sigh for it.

"Human interest," of course. Vast reading publics rise to its bait.

Editors recognize it the instant they encounter it. Readers know it, usually without knowing why.

Human interest. Put it into the test tube, study it under a slide, feel it between your thumb and forefinger. That is, if you can capture it.

Human interest. It is the quality that makes Becky Sharpe linger in your mind long after you have forgotten the plot of *Vanity Fair*. It is what David Harum had, and Ibsen's *Nora*. It is what makes, you remember Rochester in *Jane Eyre*. It is what causes you to ponder to yourself, "I've met that girl somewhere before!" And then you remember where. You have met her in a short-story of a magazine stand. She was created by some author with a gift of making people human and interesting.

It is the quality that sometimes inspires readers to write to authors in the following vein: "I take exception to the character of 'Butch' in your story in the current Atomic Age magazine. You not only gave him big ears, like my son, Butch, which is nasty of you, but his temper is identical with my boy's. I don't know where you can have met my child in real life, but I could certainly sue you for putting him in your story."

Or something like this is likely to come to the doorstep of the author with a flare for human interest: "I have just read your novel,

The Starry Night. I am trembling so that I can scarcely write these words. You certainly must have had me in mind, because you told my life story. And yet I know that no one knows my story except myself. I must see you.'

The following is another, type of case-in-point: "Dear Miss Hurst: I just loved your article about the old lady and her son. I will explain why I am writing to you. My mother, before she died, asked my dear old grandmother if she would take her baby and raise her like she had done by herself. So when Mama died, Grandma got adoption papers right away, and came and took me home with her, and kept me, educated and had me taught dressmaking and a little music. I have one baby-boy, two years old. He surely is a darling. When one year old, he had the croup on Christmas, and nearly died. I nursed him at that time ninety hours, he would not let anyone do anything for him-just cried for Mommie, so I have suggested to my husband, let's adopt a Grandma, that is an excuse for writing this. I am really sick I want an old lady so bad. I think why is really because my Grandma was so wonderful to me.

"She was a little red head and how I loved her.

"Now what I started is I would like the old lady's address of your story in Saturday's paper. I can give her a good home, plenty to eat if she will come, and care if she needs care.

"My husband is the herdsman on this farm we live on. He surely is one of the best men I ever knew. We never quarrel, because he surely loves Baby and me. Now I would like to know if there's any chance of getting this old lady you wrote about. I don't want her for any work, I just want a companion. We live here in the country, so neighbors, and what is, are not neighborly. So I get to thinking and get nervous, and oh if I just had a nice old lady.

"We would be so good and I know Junior-baby would love her, and call her Grandma, because I have talked so much about her that he is asking when Grandma is coming.

"My husband will go any time and bring her. In fact we will all go because he won't leave me home.

"I am enclosing a stamp for answer. We will take care of everything she needs. Clothes and etc. Hoping to hear from you soon, I am, sincerely yours..."

Human interest. What has it to do with the survival quality of novels, plays, even poetry. We remember Lysistrata, Canterbury

Tales, Lady Macbeth, the Three Guardsmen, Micawber, Trilby, Rowena, Nana, Little Eva, Carol Kennicott, for reasons of their human interest. Their motives and actions are akin to our own. We understand them. Human interest, like Greek drapery, is timeless, ageless, and does not come into, or go out of fashion.

Obviously, this quality which lifts human beings off the printed page in full dimension, is more than just the ability to stick a pair of big ears on the right "Butch." Somewhere between the author's muscle known as his heart, and the convoluted mass known as his brain, resides that ability to create and arouse human interest.

Yet who can possibly analyze the geniuses who succeeded in creating this procession of living fiction characters: Tom Jones. Sancho Panza. Don Quixote. Baron Munchhausen. Hedda Gabbler. Pendennis. Hamlet, Pygmalion. Babbitt. Huckleberry Finn.

These imaginary characters have blood, not ink, in their arteries. And that moment when the elixir of life begins to move in the veins of a character is the moment in which even the average author experiences one of those fleeting ecstasies of creative accomplishment. And only an author, however mediocre, can know the excitement of this strange alchemy taking place beneath his pen.

When we stand in front of Michaelangelo's David, or develop pain-in-the-neck, beneath the Sistine ceiling, we are not primarily concerned with the artist's tremendous pangs of tremendous birth. But somewhere along the line, as these masterpieces took shape, the creator was receiving his unique compensation, in terms that transcend material reward.

People are prone to ask the average author such average questions as these: Do you take your characters from real life? Do you travel around a great deal for your local color? How do you choose your subjects? Is your story clearly outlined in your mind before you begin work? Do you rewrite a great deal?

After I have replied to these various questions, there is always the uneasy feeling that only the least of it has been said. The queries are easy enough to answer concretely, but somehow they do not convey the processes.

Thus: With few exceptions I do not take my characters from real life. Almost invariably they are the result of composite impressions of many people rolled into one. Do I travel about a great deal for local color? I travel about considerably, but seldom with the concrete idea of turning up a situation, or a character, in order to incorporate him or her into fiction. Certainly I do not deliberately go out in search of that elusive end-of-the-rainbow known as human interest.

Usually, I do not choose my subjects at all. They choose me. For instance, I wrote my novel, "Lummox," because every time I passed a charwoman on her knees scrubbing a hallway, or hurried by a figure hovering in a tenement vestibule, the invitation to write a story of these inarticulate people who move along the fringes of the daily scene, was repeated.

A common technique, of course, of some authors is to choose subjects closely related to the contemporaneous scene. Or, in reverse, there is the author who prefers the historic scene of yesteryear. I never have written an historical novel. Neither do I follow the lead of topical subjects of the hour.

The structure of a story is clearly outlined in my mind from basement to attic, before I begin to work. It is as well defined in my imagination, as an architect's plans on his blueprint. To be sure, I sometimes deviate in the writing. A young woman in my novel, "Hallelujah," began to lose ground with me as I was writing her. I worried about her when I was away from my typewriter. I was not happy about her when I was in front of it. Then one day my difficulty became clear. I needed a character with whom I had not reckoned in by blueprint of the story. Or rather, she needed him. Getting him born into the story, solved her problems and mine.

Yes, I rewrite a great deal, although there are those who hold that the delicate art of writing can be spoiled by too much rewriting. Be that as it may, I usually do a novel of one hundred thousand words, over two or three times. This applies also to the short story.

I systematize my work, beginning at eight in the morning, and remaining at my desk about six hours daily. Sometimes the page on which I started is still in the typewriter at the end of the day. Again I may have two or three thousand words to show for the lonely driving hours.

And yet, answering these concrete questions concretely, does not succeed in conveying in full, the assembling processes of writing a story or movie.

40

"Local" color is frequently a misnomer for "human interest."The former can be applied as superficially as a cornice to a building. It is the result of an author's ability to inject into a scene or a personality, little touches that are as true to life as a good documentary picture of a pretty girl and her kitten.

I once spent several months in Hawaii. While there I was struck by the immense popularity of a friend of mine. An American columnist, the late O. O. McIntyre.

Honolulu virtually began its day on O. O. McIntyre. People telephoned to one another after breakfast: Did you see what McIntyre had to say this morning? One big industrialist, a pineapple magnate with a hobby for growing orchids on his immense estate, kept an O. O. McIntyre filing cabinet.

Naturally, when I returned to New York I relayed all of this to Odd McIntyre himself.

Well, one day, several months later, I received a present from the pineapple-magnate in Hawaii, a great hamper of his beautiful home-grown orchids. But the orchids themselves were not the major excitement. Rather, it was the fact that they had arrived in New York via the first non-stop airplane flight ever made from Honolulu to the mainland.

Because of the pineapple magnate's admiration for Odd McIntyre, and because of the circumstances of their transportation, I sent half of my orchids to McIntyre, with an explanatory note about the nonstop flight.

Now, I am sure that your guess would be precisely what mine was as to what McIntyre would write in his column. Nothing of the sort. Odd McIntyre apparently knew his human interest better than I did. And so, did he describe the fact that his orchids had arrived by way of the first non-stop flight from Honolulu to the mainland? He did not. What he noted, was the fact that he had received a letter from me, and letters from me always amused him, because in addressing the envelopes, I draw little faces in the capital "O's" which made up his initials. Human interest! Somewhere embedded in McIntyre's selective process, was the reason why he was bible to so many millions of American readers.

Just a few weeks ago I read a book review which was a classical example of the application of local color, as opposed to the wider implications of human interest. Said local color was applied by Old Master, Bernard Shaw. He was reviewing a biography of Beatrice

Webb, famous wife and collaborator of Sidney Webb. Both of them belong to the foremost historians of England, are leaders in the Fabian movement and experts in Russian political, and economic, life.

Well, Shaw not only analyzed their erudition, their highly skilled investigations, their political economy. His review was also a brilliant analysis of a married-couple known as Mr. and Mrs. Sidney Webb. Shaw took time out to tell how Beatrice Webb would suddenly leave off working beside her husband, in order to shower him with embraces. Shaw took time off in the midst of his interpretation of the mental scope of the writing Webbs, to explain that they were the most inveterate pair of talkers he had ever known. Next, without any particular reason for it, Shaw launched into a recital of Sidney Webb's habit of fainting occasionally, without symptoms or signals of any kind.

Thus, by a few swift strokes of fingerpainting, Shaw applied local color to material that might otherwise have remained rigidly in the realm of routine book-reviewing.

Many an editor who recognizes his human interest writer, as a wine-taster recognizes his product, will say to an author, "I wonder if you feel like doing a story about this fellow who bought the Atlantic Ocean the other day. There is a lot of human interest in the way his divorced wife backed him up in the purchase." Or perhaps he'll say: "Folks are especially interested in home-life these days. The return of the soldier, and the future home he plans with his bride, is packed with human interest. What about a story along these lines?" Likewise, human interest can be the kiss of life to many subjects that ordinarily fall outside the realm of fiction.

Socrates had a chummy colloquial approach to his profound discussions. He not only sat on the curbstone but he talked to the man on the street in his own idiom.

Human interest is a great leavener. It brings subjects, frequently outside the interest of the man on the street, closer to his range. Shakespeare was a past master of this. Lofty poet, erudite philosopher, he kept the pedestrian-quality because he was pedestrian himself. He may not have written down to the masses, but he certainly wrote for them.

Now, to be sure, unless with all this; an author has wings to his spirit, his rank as an artist will remain low. Mere skill in local color is only a handmaid to creative writing.

Pulp magazines are filled with writers who can adequately camouflage with local color. So are the comic-strips. But the Galsworthys, the Thomas Hardys, the Tolstoys are the realists who have wings to their spirit. They are the Rembrandts, the Michaelangelos of literature.

But to get back to human interest as applied to reader interest. Whatever its chemistry, whatever its source, it is the ingredient that brings the flush of life to writing. It is the ingredient which caused that woman to write: Why did you use my Butch in your story, even to his big ears?

There were two things that really stuck with me in this article.
1.   It is important that the people in your story are interesting.
2.   Little things are extremely important in making the people interesting

This reminds me of a concept I learned as "The Significant Detail." The idea is that an author can convey a wealth of information about a person or place by mentioning a single, if it's the right one. For it to be significant, that detail is either unexpected or just plain awesome, and it gives an impression of the subject as a whole. You don't need to run a laundry list describing every little thing. For instance, the author of this article draws faces in the O's of a man's name. That detail leads me to make a plethora of assumptions about her personality and their relationship as a whole. In her words this type of detail adds "Human Interest."

I think that's what Fannie is driving at here. Those little, specific details can make your characters memorable.

It's All A Matter of Timing

By Nelson S. Bond

Nelson S. Bond wrote several dozen pulp stories and was published by a wide variety of magazines, including Blue Book, Fantastic Adventures, Weird Tales, Esquire *and* Amazing Stories. *He also wrote for radio and television.*

This article comes from the October, 1940 issue of Writer's Digest.

Prominent in this story is a formula for a short story, similar to the Lester Dent Pulp Master Fiction Plot, which can be found all over the internet. This story formula is a little more general purpose than Dent's formula.

I t's the damnedest thing! I stand up there with my heart full of hope and my mitts full of driver; I wiggle and I waggle; I straighten my left arm and lower my head; I haul my hips back. I swing. My clubhead goes *swoosh!* - and the ball goes *ploop!* A one hundred and fifty yard drive. Fifty up, fifty down, and fifty yards into the lush tangle of crab grass between the tee and the fairway.

My companion says, "Tsk," and stares after my ball thoughtfully. "You going after it?" she asks. "Be careful. There's lions and tigers in there!"

She takes her stance. She's tiny and slim, and her hands are soft. She weighs 106 in her Kaysers. Her biceps are about as tough and sinewy as a cup custard. She swings. A gentle little swaying motion. But the club head goes *splat!* against the ball. Said pill takes off like a homing pigeon; soars high and far and true, and comes to rest at long last, gleaming whitely upon the green bosom of the fairway halfway to the pin.

Why? I weigh more than she does. I'm taller. I'm stronger. My clubs are heavier.

I f I wrote like I golf, there wouldn't be any long, lazy, blood-pressure-raising afternoons on the links. There would be handouts and patched breeches and truckloads of rejection slips. But by some quirk of fate-possibly because the gods have a celestial budget to balance-I am so lucky as to possess, in my vocation, that which I can't grasp when I'm playing. A sense of timing.

I'm not sure that I can tell you what it is, or how to do it. I suspect it's One of Those Things, like swimming or swinging a golf club or knowing that the third Scotch-and is enough.You have it or you don't. If you don't, you just keep on plugging, going through the motions, until one day, suddenly, there it is and you know what I'm talking about.

And when you've got it, you're sitting pretty. Meat On the table, checks in the poke, and luh-huv in my heart for yoo-hool

You're bound to get it, too, if you keep working at it. You know the old gag about how "every writer has to get a million lousy words out of his system." Of course, that's the old malarkey. Some writers click on the first go-round, others (like myself) have to do it the hard way. The truth remains, though, that those first, feeble, fumbling attempts are valuable. Every word you put on paper is another lesson in writing. Even if the story comes bouncing back with the stamps still moist, you've learned something from it. Maybe you've just learned how *not* do it next time. And, buddy, if you have-that's valuable!

Did I hear a snarl in the audience? You want me to skip the fight-talk, huh? Get down to business? All right. You're asking for it. Here's my theory on the way to "time" a normal, 5,000 word story in such a way as to make it fast, dramatic and salable.

I don't guarantee it; I don't claim that all other methods are wrong. I believe, with Kipling, that "there are six-and-twenty and ways of constructing tribal lays . . . every single one of them is right!" All I say is that this works for me.

DESIGN FOR BRICKLAYING A STORY
(Patent not worth applying for)

General Instructions

Lay out approximately 20-25 sheets of clean, white paper. I prefer Corrasable Bond because it actually does-as Arnold Gingrich of Esquire puts it-"take erasure with dignity." And an ordinary pencil eraser, to. If the Eaton People want to send me a check for this plug, I'm not proud. Use the 16, rather than the 20 pound weight. It costs less, and keeps down the postage.

Lay out an equal amount of yellow "second sheets," a piece of carbon paper, your cigarettes and matches-*Hold it!* Change that typewriter ribbon! Your chances of selling fade in direct proportion to the fading of your ink, friend! Now put that damned thesaurus away. Hide it! If you don't know the words and use them in your ordinary conversation, they'll bulge in your story like an olive in a snake's gut.

We'll take it for granted you know how to title and identify your manuscript. If you don't you shouldn't be reading this; you should be studying back issues of Writer's Digest. Name and address in upper left corner, approximate number of words in upper right, title and your name halfway down the page. All right! Let's go!

First 1000 Words. **Ends on Page 5.**

Get going with a bang! Remember, you're writing a short story, not *Gone With the Wind.* You can't waste words, nor will the editor permit you to waste his or the readers' time. Your first thousand words must tell *who* are to be the central characters of this work-of-art, *when* the story takes place, *where* the scene is set, *what* the problem is, and set the question as to how the hero expects to take care of it.

Get me straight! I don't mean you should start off anything like this-

"John Marmaduke Frasier, tall, blonde and handsome Sheriff of Burp's Crossing, Arizona, strode down Main Street wondering what he should do about saving the property of his fiancée, sweet Hildegarde Phlewzy, from the clutches of rich bank president, Phineas Gelt, who threatened to foreclose the mortgage on August 19th, 1904, twenty days hence . . ."

IT'S ALL A MATTER OF TIMING

You think I'm crazy, eh? Nobody ever introduced a story that way? Guess again! I sat beside Harry Widmer of Ace Publications for a full hour one afternoon, reading over his shoulder unsolicited manuscripts that opened in exactly that fashion. Needless to say, the stories were not offered by "regulars," nor did they come in the folders of an agent. They were the "unrush" mail, i.e., the free-lance offerings that earn pale blue slips reading, "We regret to say-"

But get the thing moving. Start with something happening to somebody; not with mental maunderings, Grab your hero by the neck and shove him smack into a mess of trouble. Then show who started that trouble-and why. Introduce the other persons involved in the problem, make their opening speeches depict their characters. As you write, keep an eye on your page numbers. Remember that this phase of the story must be finished by the middle of page 5.

End the opening sections with the implication that Our Hero recognizes his difficulty and knows what he's going to do about it.

Second 1000 words. Ends on Page 9-10.

This is the phase wherein Our Hero's star is in the ascendency. Things move along with reasonable assurance of eventual success. Looks like the problem wasn't so terrible after all. With matters moving smoothly, this section may also be used for brief, telling "flashbacks" (if required), and for strengthening characterizations.

A word about scene changes. Many beginning writers seem to go haywire over time and place transitions. That's simply because they make an easy job tough for themselves. For instance, We've all seen manuscripts in which a character leaves a room, goes to another place, meets other people. The beginner, his "timing" hopelessly off, tries to follow the character all the way-

"He stalked from the building indignantly, found a taxi at the door, rode uptown, got out at his own apartment, paid off the cabby, took the elevator upstairs..."

Sharper-edged, neater and vastly more readable is a device used by all professionals and editors. The bridging of time by a quadruple space. Finish one scene. Slap your space-lever twice-and begin your new section with a scene as fresh, as new, as clean-cut as if you were starting an entirely new story!

Here's the way it works in actual practice. Scene one was in the apartment of a detective, Sid ("Softy") O'Neill. A policeman has come to bring Softy to headquarters. The first scene ends and the second scene begins as follows.

"Okay, let's go!" (said Softy.) Then he remembered and jerked open a drawer in his desk. Dull blue glinted as he jammed something into a harness beneath his left arm-pit. "Let's go!" he repeated.

The Chief said, "Gentlemen, meet Detective O'Neill. Sid is not a member of the city force, but as I told you . . ."

It is not until some paragraphs later that the Chief is introduces by name, or the second phase of the plot determined. But story stuff is unimportant here; we are concerned only with the question of time-and-place transitions. During the blank space left above, Softy O'Neill presumably covered a number of city miles and consumed a half hour's time. The reader is made conscious of that by implication. You don't have to drag him along the route with you. How Softy got to headquarters is unimportant; all that matters is that he got there! Save words, save time. It's all a matter of timing!

Third 1000 words. Ends on Page 13-15.

Here's where the Hero stubs his toe. Things looked good-now the Villain heaves a monkeywrench onto the woiks! Trouble-with a capital "Boo!"-pops up. Technically this is known as a "plot complication." Which is just a literary way of saying it's a, "Dood Dod, what do I do now?" mess.

Let's backtrack a moment and dovetail this. We'll suppose our story to have been (1) sports, (2) science-fiction, (3) detective, (4) love, (5) romantic adventure. Show how a "complication" piles on the major problem in each of the aforementioned.

1. Hero flashy player, without his team cannot win championship vital to athletic future of small college. In phase one, main problem set forth. In phase two, path looks easy-hero going like house afire. Phase three, complication-vital blocking back busts leg before crucial game!

2. Hero hastily finishing spaceship with which to visit Mars; must get special Martian desert weed to stave off dreadful scourge which threatens to destroy Earth. Complication. Enemy scientists corners market on beryllium, vitally essential metal for construction of spaceship. . Detective hero hunting Red Jornegan, gangster,

whose fingerprints were found all over gun that murdered cop. Tracks Jornegan to hide-out. *Complication.* Finds Jornegan dead, *killer's gun lying across room with Jornegan's fingerprints on it!* (Whew! This one came off the top of my mind. I wonder whodunit?)

3. Hero admires movie idol, wangles introduction, succeeds in making him veddy, veddy interested. Soft odor of orange blossoms in distance, and then-*complication!* Learns his contract has a nix-wedding-bells clause.

4. Hero, Foreign Legion lieutenant, besieged by a mob of howling Bedouins. Must carry news of uprising to post. Remembers cache of ammunition in desert. Finds it. *Complication.* Bullets are for different rifle!

In short, then, this complication is generally something he did not nor could have possibly expected; it may even be a break the villain himself did not count on. But it makes a heluva situation for Our Hero.

Fourth 1000 words. Ends on Page 17-19.

Herein, two things happen. The Hero, finds, thinks, or fights his way out of the complication. This consumes almost all of the fourth phase. And when we've suffered with him, bled him into open country again-

Up pops the Villain with his deepest, most dastardly plot, unfolded, finally, in all its dire ramifications!

This is the trouble! Ossa on Pelion, if youse lugs know what I mean. This is the spot wherein (in the ancient mellerdramers) Nick Carter used to get two busted legs and a broken back, while a horde of savages armed with scythes and swords and Stuka bumbers swarmed in on him.

That won't go today-thank heaven! I've heard too much poppycock and balderdash about how "the pulps *demand* an excess of emotion." Action, yes! True emotion, yes! But in my opinion, they neither want, nor will buy, blatantly overwritten mellerdrama.

Anyway, that's a good rule to go buy. Figure it this way and you can't go far wrong-the only reason pulps print hokey stuff is that sometimes they can't get the smooth kind of writing they'll grab when it's offered to them. Let a man learn his trade, and he'll be snatched up by the slicks in a split-second. I think none of the following ex-pulpateers will object if I mention their names in passing: William R. Cox, who has parlayed his *Dime Sport* muscle men into *American, Liberty, et al.* Ernest Haycox, who sells super-Westerns to every top-ranking magazine and to Hollywood. Richard Sale . . . Jacland Marmur . . . WIlliam Fay . . . but why go on? Their stories had what it takes; they've moved up (Yeah, yeah, I know, they still sell some to the pulps!) and others can profit by studying their techniques.

Some digression. We were in Phase Four, where Our Hero is up to his neck in Trouble. And the Villain is on the bank, heaving rocks at his head.

How to get him out? That's your problem, pal! If I knew, I'd write the story, not donate the outline. But there are several sturdy, tried-and-true methods. By his superior knowledge. By a quirk of chance *carefully planted* in the earlier part of the story (none of that long arm of coincidence stuff)! By sheer fighting ability.

And he accomplishes this in-

The Fifth 1000 words. Ends on Page 21-25.

This is the phase of the solution, of final explanation, of *denouement*. In the detective story, here's where your cop or shamus explains whodunit, why, and how he figured it out. In the western, science, sport or action story, this is where Our Hero fights free and, tying up loose ends, explains to his public how he knew just what to do.

The fifth phase of begins with violent action, tears along swiftly, leading to a swift, decisive conclusion-and ends happily.

Watch your timing here! Pace your final conflict so that the action of it consumes approximately 500 words or more. Previous action may have been truncated to move the story along-but not this final scene. Your readers have suffered with the Hero for 4,000 words. Give 'em a blow-by-blow description of the Last Stand, let their empathies jump with glee as the Villain flinches, cowers, and dies.

I could mention a half dozen writing "tricks" that arouse this emphatic feeling, but there's no time to do so in this article. Nor is this the proper place to do it. This is simply a blueprint, a method of mechanically plotting the short story, that has worked for me-and it will work for you, if you'll give it a trial.

If you'll hew to the page-markers set forth here, I think you'll have no more trouble with tedious openings, long, drowsy middle sections, stories that refuse to end. Because writing-like that confounded golf swing I cannot master-is all a matter of timing.

Oh, I said that before, didn't I? Well-it still goes!

Here's a recap of this general purpose short story formula:

1. *First 1000 words.* Introduce everything, protagonist, setting, mood and the story's main problem.
2. *Second 1000 words.* Protagonist set out to solve the story problem, and finds initial success.
3. *Third 1000 words.* Protagonist comes across a complication or a major setback.
4. *Fourth 1000 words.* Protagonist pays the price, does the work and sets thing in place.
5. *Fifth 1000 words.* Protagonist has final confrontation with complication/villain, then receives a just reward.

GET THAT NOVEL OUT OF YOUR SYSTEM

By Marjorie Holmes

This article sounds like it was written after Marjorie Holmes's first book. She ended up writing 134 books, 32 of which hit the bestseller list. She also wrote for all manner of magazines. From Writer's Digest, August 1943.

Once you've written that novel that's in you, crying to be written, you can live with yourself again. You can face your image in the mirror without flinching. You can sleep nights.

You'll never be satisfied to dismiss it in a few pages as The Novel I Didn't Write. A matter of personal integrity is involved. If it's peculiarly and fiercely your novel, no one else *can* write it but you. And if you're at all serious about your work, you're in for self-inflicted hell until you do!

Writing a novel is so long a task, so perilous a gamble. The free-lancer must stake so much valuable writing time against monstrously uncertain success. In that same period he knows he can be turning Out many shorter manuscripts, making a go of Writing.

But unless the "good book" in the back of the mind of every writer is actually written, he fears that always he will be a hack Writer, at odds with himself and the people who have had faith in him.

But-and here looms the most sinister threat of all-*what if he does gamble all on his novel and then it doesn't sell?* He realizes that, in that eventuality, he can no longer take refuge even in his dreams. He will be shocked and wounded; he will not only be far behind the eight-ball financially, but he will probably be conditioned for good against the novel form... And so, while you are tormented by the knowledge that you're compromising, shirking your task, the cold sick dread of failure is holding you back. Mentally and emotionally you are a mess!

This is the story of the novel I did write. Things that affected the slow, agonized crawl to its completion. Maybe there's something in it for you?

I began my novel shortly after I was out of college. The stimulus was a series of remarkable articles by Clark Venable, which the WRITER's DIGEST ran from February through July, 1933. "Subject Matter and Beginning," "The Voice of Jacob," "Characterization," "Color and Tempo," even "The Last Hard Mile." (They were wonderful!) I gulped down Mr. Venable's advice, gave myself the tests: "Am I equipped to tell this story? Have I the dogged determination required for the chore? Is my story worth the labor and will it justify the use of the equipment I will bring to it? If all answers are definitely yes," Mr. Venable urged, "then in heaven's name *begin*."

And so, gasping a frantic yes, yes! to all of them, in heaven's name I-began. In heaven's name I wrote, furiously, gloriously, for weeks. Then one sad day I paused for breath and looked back. To my stunned amazement, I found it had taken me 90,000 words to simply set the stage! Actually, I knew nothing about writing the novel. Even Mr. Venable's fine articles assumed an experience and technical background I did not have.

I would have to put this material away. I would have to start at the bottom with stories and articles. I would have to learn structure and dramatic balance and discipline. I would have to mature.

It was a bitterly disappointing decision to have to make, but I knew it was the only way.

At that time I had sold a couple of pulp and confession stories. To these I gratefully and hopefully returned. I painstakingly built plot outlines; I polished and tested every page.

Sometimes, angrily throwing away the tenth version of a dramatic scene, I would protest, "What's the difference? The editors will probably cut. And it's just a confession, isn't it?" But I could never kid myself. And I believe that this habit of petting, and practically tasting every sentence, every word, before letting it go, made for the kind of writing that had to go into my book. The book that I was still working on-simply because I couldn't resist it-now and then.

To get my name into the more general magazines, I was also writing fluff. Airy little articles about love, glamor, personality, husbands, kids. These were easy to write and sold readily. I got anywhere from $10 to $75 for them, with frequent reprint bonuses which made the total take for the time involved very good. Together with story sales I made sometimes as much as $800 a month. I was in a (very small) unspectacular way, doing all right.

But-I couldn't sleep nights. I'd read articles like Steve Fisher's "Literary Roller Coaster" and walk the floor. Why, the guy was only 25 While I-well, let's skip that. Anyway, I was old enough to have finished my book too if I'd just quit stalling, if I just had the courage to drop everything else and see it through. In a kind of panic, I'd open my notebook to the words an English prof had scribbled there once: "You can write beautiful things for people who crave beautiful things. There is a duty!" Or I'd gaze wretchedly at Clark Venable's closing paragraph, clipped, framed, and hung over my desk: "For aught any man can say to the contrary, the author of that greatest novel may be now a lowly beginner who has within him the seed of genius which flowers only when WORKED. You?..."

In spasms like this I would haul down my novel, which despite the infrequent spurts on which I had worked on it, had grown to surprising proportions, and brood over it. I felt that I really had something in it; that, if nothing more, I had captured the spirit of a kind of people I wanted to portray. But something was wrong-and I didn't know just what. I was too close to it, perhaps too much in love with it to regard it with an objective, discerning eye. Finally, though I'd never had much faith in critics, I bundled it up and sent it off to Mr. A. L. Fierst.

Money was never more luckily spent. I already knew that the book was too long, but I was lost and confused in determining what to cut. He pointed out what must go-and why. He suggested a plan for complete reorganization. In one letter he taught me things about writing a novel that I'll remember all my life.

One mistake I had made was in the number of characters. I love characterization. My idea of creative bliss would be to write nothing but character sketches till the end of time. This I had been doing with the excuse that I was writing a novel. Every amusing or colorful character I had ever observed and "canned" in my notebook, had been lovingly dusted off and shoved onto a stage where he served no particular purpose and had no business to be. The result was a bizarre collection of personalities, each interesting in itself, perhaps, but contributing nothing to the plot, and only obscuring the true protagonists.

It was these few principal characters who were really important. On their backs rested the plot. It was through their courage, loyalty, and rollicking spirits that I must accent the theme. They deserved the spotlight, the very best that I could give them. To do this I couldn't go dashing down bypaths, exploring the morals of the town drunkard, deciding what the garbage man thought about.

And once I had-however regretfully-killed off all these other minor characters, I had not only shortened the book considerably, but gained elbow-room to build up the characters I was really interested in. The Andrews family itself, and the few people who contributed to their destiny. This simplified the problem, the story, and the mood. It made for dramatic unity. It quickened the pace.

To further quicken the pace, I did what I should have done in the beginning-made chapter outlines, as if each were a short story in itself, leading to a dramatic climax. Then I went through every chapter already written, trying to shape it over the skeleton of this outline. A lot of irrelevant scenes had to be lifted out bodily-some of them to be discarded completely, others to be salvaged and worked into different chapters where they more aptly fit. For instance, in the original version of the manuscript, I had scattered the theatrical experiences of Ken, the older brother, through four or five chapters dealing with other matters. In revising, I gathered them all together and sewed them into a couple of chapters all his own, where they belonged.

In making these tardy chapter outlines, I discovered chapters that seemed dramatically out of place. These I shifted around until-like those little dime-store puzzles where you tilt and twist until the darkie's eyes or teeth fall into place-they seemed to fit. To illustrate, I tried the chapter where the kitchen catches on fire, at least four different places. But not until I arranged so that it should follow a chapter dealing with the family's difficulties at Christmas, did it live up to its own dramatic implications.

Timing, in the modern novel, is important. Almost as important as in a short story, I think. Speaking for the moment as simply a reader, I am distressed at how often novelists pay no attention to it. A dramatic effect achieved, a point made they often still go wordily on, to ruin that effect. I'm wordy enough myself, heaven knows! But the precaution of a chapter outline, pointing to a definite curtain line or peak of interest at which to stop, is a safeguard against going too far afield, as well as invaluable as a timing device.

Another mistake I made in first writing my novel was in handling the dialogue. My own short story experience should have taught me that dialogue serves two purposes-to delineate character and advance the plot. But somehow I got the notion that in novels no such hampering limitations prevailed. I love to write dialogue, and so I had a grand time letting everybody talk their heads off. They argued, they dissertated, they philosophized. And while a lot of it made interesting reading in itself, it kept the characters marking time when they should have been going someplace. A novel-as Mr. Venable had warned-must march!

Perhaps the over-abundance of dialogue had been due to my anxiety to make my characters realistic. I had faithfully reproduced pages of conversation authentic to a certain kind of people. Every interruption and half-speech, every "huh?" "gosh, kid," "I dunno" and "damn." The result had used up a lot of space (you haven't nearly as much elbow-room in a novel as you might imagine-the pasture looks vast and green after the narrow roads of short story writing, but that's where so many of us go astray). More disastrously, it had become so realistic as to defeat its own end. The oral word is a tricky thing when reproduced in print. For instance, if I were to take down literally the conversation that took place recently at a luncheon, I would succeed only in making a group of refined ladies sound like a bunch of bawdy madams. Similarly, in my novel, the dialogue of typical, small-town middle-class girls, too conscientiously recorded, gave the impression that they were tawdry and cheap, instead of the nice, appealing youngsters they were. This dialogue had to be pared down and cleaned up. Since my novel wasn't to be hairy-chested Steinbeck or Hemingway realism, anyhow, dialogue that went all out for realism threw the thing out of balance; actually giving it an unrealistic effect. Rather than impairing the ultimate realism–the stuff that makes a reader feel that he sees and knows the places described, participates in the story-a realism that, thank heaven, the critics are agreeing is there-I believe that my willingness to compromise a little with realism, contributed to its final achievement

In other words, the novelist, like the painter, must sort over his material, using only that part of it essential to the design he has in mind-and often streamlining and simplifying even that.

While on the subject of realism, you might like to know something about my methods of capturing it. This will take us back for a moment to characterization. Most people agree that the scene stealer in *World by the Tail*, is Sam, a cocky, witty, infuriating little clown of a dad, so let's take a look at him. Better, let's look at the strip of paper that was long pinned over my desk, labeled-SAM.

Physical Characteristics:
- short, fat tummy, bald-headed
- big nose
- ruddy complexion
- fat lips-wrinkled, like prunes
- devilish blue eyes
- likes snappy clothes
- traces of powder on his ear lobes after shaving.
- ... etc.

Mannerisms:
- thumbing his suspenders
- slapping his knee
- noisily blowing his nose
- pointing foolishly to his bald head
- ... etc.

Pet speech tags:
- "Never did like ya very good, any way-"
- "Don't y'know it is?"
- "Cheer up, Christmas is comin', ain't it???
- ... etc.

I didn't remember or think up all these characteristics at once; they came to me as I brooded over the character, recalling or observing them. The list grew along with the story. But having it within glancing distance kept Sam always vividly strutting and chuckling and kicking up his heels before me. I couldn't lose sight of him, consequently he came vividly out of the typewriter.

I kept sheets like that for every one of the characters-Jean, Ken, Polly-all of them. Such lists helped me to visualize and get hold of the characters I wasn't quite sure about. And they prevented me from being so mentally sure of a character that I failed to portray him on paper, where the reader could see and know him, too.

The realism of your settings is important. I know the small, Midwestern lake town background intimately, but every time I go back to it I fill my notebook with homely little details never recorded there before. The shaggy, mashed-down look of dock posts, the melancholy dip of rowboats at anchor, the dried foam looking like snow upon the sand. Dusty little towns with their jutting flagpoles at the corner of main street, ordering *inside turn...* small town hostesses reminding pertly, "Save your fork," as they serve the pie... the look and smell of a hayloft in late afternoon-. Those are the kind of things that go into my notebook. Then when I'm miles from the Midwest but trying to write about it, I have at my fingertips all the warm, pungent, vivid details that will recreate the scene.

But in the use of realistic detail, as in all else, I learned that the novelist must not overplay his hand. Background must remain just that-background. It must not be so glowing as to detract from the color of the characters. It must not hold up the action. Any vast ornate chunks of it must be broken up and scattered throughout the scene.

Figures of speech also pepper my notebook. Everything I see seems to remind me of something else. It's fun to discover unique ones, and I am perhaps overfond of using them. One reviewer said my novel starts off as if I had "contracted with Reader's Digest to supply its Picturesque Speech department for the season" before I settle down to telling the tale. I shall remember that next time. Too many similes can be too much cake.

Another mistake I made in my first floundering attempts at writing a novel, was failure to clarify the theme. Frankly, I hadn't considered that I was writing a "theme novel"—that is, a book to prove anything. I was interested only in showing a certain kind of people for the gay, courageous souls they were. What I had failed to realize was that by their gaiety and courage they were proving something-if I could just fasten on what that was, make all episodes, however subtly, point to it, draw it out. I reread novels that I had loved for their characterizations deliberately refusing to be charmed away from that binding thread-the theme. However well hidden, it was always there!

Well, I thought about this theme business a lot during the three years that my novel lay around the house untouched. You see, shortly after receiving my criticism of this first version and getting all steamed up to revise, there were complications on the home front. I was going to have a baby. It seemed a very poor time to turn my back on all the money I could be making free-lancing. Besides, I began to be plagued by all those doubts mentioned at first. What if I gave up my markets, gambled a year or two on my novel, and then it didn't sell? I just didn't have the nerve. Perhaps-now keenly aware of its many faults, and quailing at the staggering amount of work involved-I was discouraged. I had lost faith.

And so I went back to free-lancing, writing everything under heaven-confessions, articles, verse, juveniles, pulps. I collaborated on booklengths with Mary Frances Morgan, that clever, attractive gal who never fails. We made a lot of money. We had a lot of fun. But after a while I began to have that harried look again. And again-I couldn't sleep nights. I'd lie awake thinking about my novel, figuring it out. I began to sneak a day or two Out of my busy schedule to work on it. But I'd just get going strong when a hurry-up, sure-money assignment would come in to lure me away from it. That would be followed by another-it would be weeks, months, before I could come back.

Finally I couldn't stand it any longer. I decided to get that novel out of my system—however swiftly, however poorly I wrote it, to get it done! I dropped everything else-sent back assignments, telling the editors the baby was keeping me busy (and he was). But even taking care of a new baby, an older child and the house didn't seem so hard when I was doing the work I wanted to do-and now felt that I was ready for. I had had ample time to ponder over the mistakes I had first made; I corrected them. I had learned a lot more about story structure; I applied it to my book. I had gotten a grip on my theme. Whatever my impatience, habits of slow, painstaking writing were not to be thrown overboard. I fought every sentence to a finish. I let nothing go until it was right.

Finally, amazingly, the thing was done. Relieved, almost incredulous, I typed the final word. It might still be a punk book, but by golly, it was a whole one! Whole and balanced out this time in a sense that satisfied.

I sent it off to my agent and forgot about it. It was wonderful just to have it out of the house. I hoped that even if nobody bought it (and somehow I could scarcely conceive that they would) he would never send it back. Consequently it was the biggest shock of my life to arrive in Pittsburgh last summer (after moving up from Texas) and find a letter from my agent, saying the Lippincott editors would like a luncheon date to talk about the book!

I went to Philadelphia with a feeling of dazed incredulity. I came home sort of drifting on bubbles and stars. But I had to get my feet back on the ground and keep them there. There was a lot of cutting to be done, and I had to cook up a new ending before they would decide. I'm terribly superstitious; I didn't risk jinxing it by telling anyone or even indulging in a dream. All I could do was work. I even wrote two new endings, so as to give the editors a choice. And fortunately so, as it was the second one they liked.

Because of my experience, I don't advise people to start their novels too soon. Don't gamble everything on your novel until you're sure you have something to say, and know how to say it. But once you're confident of that, wade in. Get it out of your system You'll never have a moment's peace until you do.

Some thoughts from this article:
- Make a list of Tag & Traits for each character (for more info on Tags and Traits, see "Butch and his Big Ears" elsewhere in this book.)
- Dialog should not sound like actual, real conversations. It should be much more to the point.
- Keep a notebook of things / descriptions that you want to put in somewhere.

PLOTTING THE SHORT-STORY

by Culpeper Chunn

This one was collected from the first 5 issues of The Writer's Monthly in 1922.

CHAPTER I - GERM-PLOTS: WHAT THEY ARE AND WHERE TO FIND THEM

A comprehensive system of plot development, and an adequate supply of material to draw from, are almost indispensable to the writer who turns out a large number of stories each year, and to the occasional scribbler who has little knowledge of plot form and structure it is of even greater value. Years of experience as a writer, literary critic and student of the short story have brought out these facts: The new writer who is "long" on writing is generally "short" on plot ideas, and an inadequate knowledge of the plot and its development causes more aspiring authors to fail than any other one thing.

Most beginners seem to have the idea that the writing game is a very easy game to play, as easy as ping-pong, for instance. Some of them have acquired a fair education; others, not so fortunate, are equipped with nothing but a gnawing desire to write, and on first appearances it seems to them that it should prove to be a very simple matter to weave their ideas into readable stories. Some of them have a vague idea of what a plot is, but they know nothing about *inciting motives, crucial situations, balance, climaxes* and other structural points, and care less. When they read in their favorite magazine a cameo-like story by some master writer, they do not realize that the author may have labored for days or weeks over that story, rearranging words, eliminating paragraphs and even whole pages from the original draft, and reconstructing the plot after he has torn it to pieces half a dozen times. The words flow so smoothly, the characters stand out so clearly, the plot is so simple— how easy it must be! But these writers are soon disillusioned when the rejection slips begin to roll in on them with the regularity of well-oiled machines. Not until they have served an apprenticeship, long or short, as may be, do they learn that authorship is as much a profession as surgery is, and that, as in all other pursuits, it is simply a matter of the survival of the fittest.

No writer can hope to achieve real success in the writing field unless he is well grounded in the fundamentals of plot construction, nor can he avoid an atmosphere of sameness in his stories and give them the stamp of cleverness and originality unless he constantly adds to his store of plot-material. The plot's the thing, and the writer who relies solely upon inspiration to furnish him with suitable plots for his stories cannot begin to compete with his more practical brother craftsman who stimulates his imagination with tidbits from real life, as it were, and builds the foundations for his stories with the same care and exactitude that a stone mason would employ in laying the foundation and outlining the framework of a house. Inspiration is, without a doubt, a very great thing, although personally I know very little about it, never having had time to sit down and wait for it to visit me. But it is a fickle creature at best, and requires as much attention as a teething baby. Even those rare exceptions among the writing fraternity who possess the divine spark need a solid base from which to start on their flights into the realms of imagery.

It is not difficult to build an occasional plot. With one girl and one man, or two girls and one man, say, for a starting point, almost any writer who has touched a few of life's high spots can build a plot of some sort, but he cannot repeat the process over and over with any great degree of success, for the reason that he must attack each new story from a different angle, and when he relies entirely upon his own limited ex perience and his imagination, he soon finds this a very difficult thing to do. For this reason experienced writers always keep on hand a varied assortment of story-ideas, original and otherwise, to be used as starting points when they make new voyages into the uncharted seas of fiction. These story ideas are called germ-plots.

A germ-plot is an idea which may be broadened out and used

as a foundation upon which to build a story—a spark, to shift the figure, that starts a conflagration in the writer's brain and makes him an object to be pitied until he sits down before his typewriter and pounds out a story to make us sit up half the night to read. Germ-plots lurk on the street corners, in dark alleys. in dingy restaurants, in ballrooms, on the faces of men and women, in the lisp of a child, in the newspapers, in magazine advertisements, in funny sayings, in love letters, in jail, in insane asylums, onboard the train, the ocean liner and the Zeppelin! The germ-plot, in short, is any original or acquired idea, unusual situation, striking title, curious advertisement, funny character, queer dream, clever story —in fact, anything that contains an element of mystery, adventure, humor, fantasy, love, etc., in which there is a twist that marks it as more or less ideal story material, and therefore legitimate plunder for the writer.

To make my meaning clearer, let me give two or three concrete illustrations. One day, several years ago, two I saw or something fall from the second-story window of an apartment house, and at first I thought that it was a man. Then a gust of wind kindly came along and opened it up and I saw that it was a pair of purple pajamas. A moment later a young lady in house attire rushed out of the house, snatched up the brilliant garment and hurried back into the house again. When I got home I promptly developed the idea into a story called "The Purple Pajamas"—and sold it.

On another occasion I saw on a bulletin board a circular advertising for an escaped convict. The line, "$500 Reward, Alive or Dead," caught my eye and started a train of thought thundering through my mind. At first glance the idea may seem trite; nevertheless, it developed into a story that I called "The Man from Virginia"-and sold.

Again: One day I read a newspaper account about a man who had a twin brother who looked so much like him that his wife, in a fit of jealous rage, shot her brother-in-law, in the belief that she was letting daylight through her husband! I nursed the idea for a couple of days, then wrote "His Brother's Keeper," and placed it without difficulty.

Every writer should have a blank book in which to jot down his germ-plots as he uncovers them. These notes are later to be neatly typed off on uniform sheets of paper and filed away for future use. Anything that seems suggestive, whether it appears to offer material for immediate use or not, should find a home in the Plot Book, where, some dark day when inspiration has taken to her heels and ideas seem to be about as plentiful as snow on the Fourth of July, it will be found waiting with a cheerful smile on its face.

To give the reader an idea of the kind of material that should be stored away, and the manner in which it is done, let me pick at random a few items from one of my many plot books:

Saw man on street today who had a scar on his face resembling a question mark. (What an idea for a story.)

Overheard a woman say: "When a man loves he will dare anything." (Suggests original title "The Man Who Dared.")

Tramp standing before the window of a fashionable restaurant gazing hungrily at the food being served within.

Saw splotch of red on a white flower in the front yard of a house today. Looked like blood.

The newspapers are a very mine of ideas for the writer, the news items, the sporting page, headings and advertisements (especially the "personal column"), all being a common stamping ground for the germ-plot. Scissors should always be kept at hand and used freely in dissecting out the interesting items one runs across when reading the papers. The shorter items and headings can then be typed off and filed away, and the longer articles pasted in a scrap book kept especially for this purpose. Consider the following headings, items and advertisements, which were actually clipped from the daily papers.

HEADINGS

- Saves Governor; Wins Pardon
- Sells Self for Life for a Pair of Shoes
- Baby Girl Left on Doorstep
- Caught Boarder Kissing His Wife
- Bride of One Day Mysteriously Murdered
- Slayer Weeps Over Victim's Body

NEWS ITEMS

(condensed)

- An unidentified white girl is found dead in a public park. Marks on the girl's throat lead police to be lieve she was murdered. Her handkerchief was marked with a number—47 (laundry mark?)
- A carrier pigeon with a broken wing fell to the ground in front of the post office and was captured by a messenger boy. A message in code was carried in a small metal cylinder tied to one leg; on the other leg was a metal band marked as follows: "HM-19373-Y."
- Two women fight in courts for possession of same baby. Both women claim to be the infant's mother. Baby was left on the a doorstep of a foundling asylum a year ago; now both women appear to claim it as their own.
- The mysterious murderer known as "Doctor X" was hung at the jail this morning. Even at the last he refused to tell his real name and it is probable his true identity will never be known.

ADVERTISEMENTS

(From "Personal Columns")

- R. L. P. Saw your message in yesterday's paper. It came to late. You must try to forget. Brown Eyes.
- Men for desperate adventure wanted. No questions asked, none expected.
- Want to communicate with a young lady matrimonially inclined. Must be a blond and willing to accompany me to South Africa.
- Jack. Come home. Sarah is dying. All is forgiven. The black box has been found. Mazie.

Where it is not practicable to preserve long accounts of murder trials and sensational robberies, jot down the clues that have enabled the detectives to run the criminals to earth. Note the following, all of which were gleaned from the columns of the newspapers, and two of which at least have been used as the central ideas around which stories have been

written:
- Broken sword-cane.
- Laundry-mark on handkerchief.
- Hairs from murderer's head clutched in victim's fingers.
- Scent of rare perfume near scene of crime.
- Imprint of murderer's teeth in apple.
- Finger-prints on dagger.

A writer should never read a magazine, novel or any other literary effort unless he has his notebook and pencil near at hand, for often he will come across a catchy phrase or an odd situation as set forth by some brilliant brother of the fraternity which will give him an idea for a story—if he can remember it when needed. Take, for example, the following suggestive lines taken for the most part from stories in current magazines:
- "Jack leaped to his feet and gazed around him wildly. The clock struck thirteen."
- "I have given you my life, my love, my wealth, myself. Can I give you more?" (Suggests original title "The Woman Who Gave Her All.")
- "He sobbed out his soul in her arms"
- "His foot was as twisted as his smile."
- "I will wear a red rose on the lapel of my coat so that you will recognize me."
- "The moon was red, as if a film of blood covered it." (Suggests title "When the Moon Shone Red.")

When a striking title occurs to you, write it down whether you think it will ever be of use to you or not. Some of the greatest short stories ever written were inspired by titles. Anyway, the day may come when you develop a plot for which you can find no suitable name. If you have a good supply of titles on hand, you will doubtless be able to find the very thing you are looking for to embellish the child of your brain. In one of my notebooks I find, among others, the following suggestive titles:
- The Devil's Prayer
- The Thirteenth Hour
- The Man Who Sneered
- The Mummy's Hand

- The Serpent's Fang
- The Kiss of Hate
- The Scarlet Halo
- The Girl in Black

Curious or striking names, too, will often prove suggestive and give us an idea that may be the means of making some joyous editor part with a substantial check. Names such as the following, for example, are well worth preserving:
- Abner Death
- Mag Scarlet
- Father Boniface
- Arizona Pete
- "Iky" Alias The (nickname for girl)
- Alias The Hawk
- Pap Lee
- Mlle. Fay

I often find it easier to build a plot around an odd character than around an odd situation, and have a separate book for Types and Characters. Types of interesting classes of people, followed by brief explanatory notes, should be entered in the book, as, for example:

CRIMINALS

- **Instinctive:** Usually those who commit crimes for the sheer love of the excitement that enters into every criminal's life. Clever criminals of this type popular with readers Arsene Lupin and the Lone Wolf good examples.
- **Occasional:** Usually average human beings of normal mentality driven to crime to by necessity, temptation, or to shield themselves or others in unusual circumstances over which they have no control.

DETECTIVES

- **Master mind:** Criminologists who solve mysteries by deduction or induction. Men of real genius in their particular line. Eccentric, with curious mannerisms, qualities.

Sherlock Holmes and the "Thinking Machine" good examples.

- **Reformed convict:** Usually a young man of some education with wide knowledge of crime and criminals. This type of detective is always popular when cleverly drawn. Cleek is a good modern example.

While I have given it but two examples in each of the foregoing classifications, it should be remembered that there are many other types of criminals and detectives, such as: (criminals) *accidental, unwilling, Oriental, low-brow or thug, etc.,* and (detectives) *scientific, crime specialist, secret service agent, police, correspondence school, etc.,* all of which are worthy of a place in the Plot Book.

In another part of the book the interesting characters one meets with should be made note of. When the characters characters one are fictional—creations of other writers—this fact should be noted, because such characters can, of course, only be used to suggest other characters of a similar type. For example:

CRIMINALS

- **Dr. Fu-Manchu.** Chinaman, cruel, crafty. Sinister motives. Deeply learned in the sciences. Highly developed mental powers. S'bilant voice. Green, filmy eyes. Cunning, more than a match for the police. Popular with readers. "The Insidious Dr. Fu-Manchu," Sox Rohmer.
- **"The Ghost."** Cracksman. Girl. Beautiful. Early history obscure. Brand on right shoulder. Disguises herself as man. Evening clothes, high silk hat, mustache, etc. Clever, daring. Matches wits with celebrated criminologist who is in love with her. (Original.)

OTHER CLASSIFICATIONS

- **Doctor:** About 30 years of age. Long and lanky. Red-headed. Fiery temper. Heart of gold. Genial and companionable at times. Something of a genious. Country practitioner. Careless obout dress, Mannerisms. Wrapped up in profession. Delays wedding to perform operation. ("Red

Pepper Burns," Grace Richmond.)

- **Mountaineer:** Rattlesnake Bill: Old, toothless, bronzed, wrinkled. Ex-feudist and moonshiner. Goes bare-footed and hatless. Wears dilapidated blue jean pants and kickory shirt. Lives in log cabin. Kindly and lovable. Biggest liar in state. Children all love him. (Original.)

I could write on in the same vein indefinitely and fill up page after page with matter of a similar character, but it is desired only to point out a few of the sources from which the writer may gather plot-material and give him an idea of the kind of material that should be preserved, and it would seem that the examples given should prove sufficient.

It is the sacred duty of every ambitious writer to acquire the notebook habit. No writer can realize the opportunities he has lost in the past, or hope to get anywhere in the future, until he does. It is a very simple matter to begin a Plot Book, and once the habit has been acquired it becomes almost second nature to jot down useful bits of information which in time will grow into a mine of inspiration for the writer who otherwise would be as barren of ideas as a creosote-dipped pup is of fleas.

In this [part] I have confined myself to explaining how to pursue, capture, and to tame the elusive idea. In articles to follow I shall endeavor to reduce the plot-construction to its most to simple form and, by developing actual plots before the reader's eyes, give him a clear understanding of plot values and show him how the embryo plots or germ-ideas can, with little trouble, be whipped into technically correct working plots.

CHAPTER II - STRUCTURE OF THE PLOT

Before we can hope to develop our germ-plots into well balanced working plots upon which to build our stories it is of course essential that we have a working knowledge of plot form and structure. A great many writers, especially beginners, are unable to round out their plots sufficiently to give their stories the proper balance, simply because they are not familiar with the technicalities of plot construction, and the author who attempts to write a story around a poorly formed plot is almost sure to find himself with an unsalable manuscript on his hands.

There are a great many writers, of course, especially among those who have "arrived," who do not find it necessary to commit their plots to paper, but work them out in their minds before they begin their stories, or build them up detail by detail after their stories are begun. To these writers, plot *balance* and *movement* have become instinctive, and they find that their words flow easier and that their imaginations are more active when they begin their stories with only a half-formed plot in mind or, indeed, with no plot at all, their theory being that the creative mental powers are given fuller play if permitted to invent while the story itself is in the process of development than if forced to form a fixed plot plan before the story has begun to materialize. But in the main these writers rely upon word-grouping (style) more than upon plot to "put their stories over," and even the best of those who adopt this policy occasionally come to grief, for it is not an easy matter to fashion a plot and beautifully formed word-groups at the same time. Such a plan, if consistently followed, usually proves fatal to the beginner. A technically correct plot upon which to build one's story is as essential to success as a thorough understanding of the language of one's country; and the only way for the novice to make sure his plots are free from technical flaws is for him to work them out on paper, according to fixed principles, with the same care that he would use in solving a knotty mathematical problem. Once the simple theories of plot construction become fixed in his mind, and he gets the *feel* of the plot, the writer can begin a story with nothing to build on but a vague idea and a burning desire, with some hope of working out a well-proportioned plot after the story is under way; but until he does master these fundamentals he courts disaster each time he begins a story unless he has worked out his plot in advance.

I venture to say that no really great short story was ever written the plot of which was not clearly outlined in the writer's mind before he began to write. Most of those writers who have exposed their methods of writing to public view have dwelt upon the importance of the plot, and many of them have explained the mechanical processes they used to build up the plots that made their stories famous. Poe, the father of the American short story, worked out the plots for his stories to a mathematical nicety, and even the framework or background of those of his stories which may be said to be devoid of plot received as much care and consideration as his more involved stories. Poe even went so far as to apply this principle to his poetry, and it may prove of interest to know that "The Raven," the most famous of his of poems, interest was, according to his own words, the result of a process of mechanics and was not, as many people believe, dashed off in the white heat of inspiration. And so it is, and ever has been since the birth of the short story proper, with most of the great writers.

The system of plot building outlined in this chapter and these to follow will, I believe, stand upon its own feet, but it should be understood that it is not designed to take the place of authoritative textbooks on this important subject. Those writers who have the leisure to do so should make an exhaustive study of the plot, calling to their aid several good treatises in order to get the teachers' points of view, and analyzing the stories they read in the current magazines so as to grasp the nature of the plot as it is handled by successful writers, and the same time become acquainted with the editorial preferences of the different periodicals. But this series of articles is aimed more particularly at the writer who has less time for reading and study, who writes only when he can snatch an hour or two from between other labors that absorb most of his time, and who has to take what instruction he can get in story writing in broken doses. The very simplicity of this system is well past the experimental stage, having been used by a number of writers with unvarying success since it was first originated by the present writer some years ago, and as it is based on the accepted principles of plot construction and offers a quick and practicable plan for applying those principles to a successful end, I venture to hope that is will prove an inspiration to those writers, beginners as well as "old timers," who will give it careful study and a thorough test.

Before taking up the actual development of plots, it is, as has been said, necessary for us to familiarize ourselves with the different parts of the plot, so that we can build the foundations for our stories on firm ground, else, like the man who built his house upon the sand, we may find the situation slipping away from us.

Let us therefore consider the following brief:

OUTLINE FOR PLOT DEVELOPMENT

General Scheme

Balance:
- Keynote.
- Crucial situation.
- Complications.
- Deliberation.
- Solution.

Movement:
1. *Direct* - Action moves tersely forward with incidents acting as index to crucial situation.
2. *Indirect* - Introducing secondary complications, crisis, etc., before the climax. Reflex of complications.

Development

Opening:
1. *Inaction* (objective)
    (a)   Introduction.
    (b)   Purely descriptive.
2. *Action*
    (a)   Revealing inciting motive.
    (b)   Theme.
    (c)   Characters.
    (d)   Setting.
    (e)   Combinations of the foregoing.
3. *Indirect action* (anticipatory)
    (a)   Suggesting inciting motive.
    (b)   Revealing theme.
    (c)   Characters.
    (d)   Setting.
    (e)   Combinations of the foregoing.

Body:
1. Incident of plot development.
2. First moment of suspense.
3. Cause of crisis.
4. Crisis.
5. Second moment of suspense.

6.   Crucial situation.
7.   Cause of climax.
8.   Climax.
Closing:
1.   Direct denouement of conclusion.
2.   Interpretation, if any.
3.   Aftermath, if any.

It will be seen that the plot is divided into three main divisions —the opening, the body, and the closing. That the foregoing outline might be complete we have given the several different openings, that of *inaction* included, though this at its best is but a poor opening and is seldom used. The crisp, well-informed plot should open either by suggesting or by revealing the inciting motive of the story. Or we may go a step farther and begin the plot with the first incident of plot development (a psychological moment, I might say), which, it will be observed, falls within the second of the three divisions. Indeed, this latter opening is usually considered the best of the three openings mentioned, because in these hurried days we do not begin a story, we start off in the middle of it, and not infrequently commence where the antiquated tale used to end. The modern reader likes to plunge directly into the action of a story, and editors, knowing this, do not as a rule look kindly upon the story with a leisurely opening.

The body, of course, is the most important part of the plot, as it serves as a frame to hold the loose threads of our idea together. The body of a model plot should be clean-cut and well-defined. Padding with unnecessary complications tends to make a plot bulky and flat unless skillfully handled. In the snappy plot, following the first incident of plot development, the writer should work smoothly, unswervingly and logically through the first moment of suspense, the cause of crisis, the crisis, and then— through the second moment of suspense, the crucial situation, and the cause of the climax— swing tersely to a climax (unless there are to be further complications). Hold to the main thread of the story idea when possible and do not leave loose strands scattered about to lead the reader astray. When complications seem desirable or necessary, try to equalize them so that the body of the plot will not lose its proper proportion.

The closing of the plot is usually restricted to the direct denouement and conclusion, for it is always best to drop to a swift end when we have disclosed our climax. Never leave the plot problem unsolved. Readers do not like to wade through a long story and then be left in doubt as to what the writer was driving at. "The Lady, or the Tiger?" type of story went out of fashion years ago, and trick stories that leave the reader guessing are taboo among editors. End a plot decisively, in such a way that explanations are unnecessary after the climax has been reached. Interpretation of a plot, which really belongs to the short story proper and has little to do with plot building, is always awkward and therefore to be avoided when practicable.

It should be borne in mind that each part of a plot has a direct bearing on the other parts and plays an important part in giving a plot *balance* and *proportion.* The building of a plot is in some respects not dissimilar to the solving of a jigsaw puzzle; each separate piece has its place and the different parts have to be fitted together with the greatest exactitude in order to obtain a complete and perfect whole. The beginner, therefore, would do well to make himself thoroughly familiar with the simple plot before experimenting with its more involved relations. Nor should this work any hardship on the writer, for the simple plot offers as many possibilities for literary accomplishment as the plot abounding in complications. Practically all of the short story classics have simple plots. Take, for instance, the stories of the three masters: Maupassant, Poe, and "O. Henry." With few exceptions these stories are written around the most simple plots, and who is there to say that this fact detracts from the absorbing interest of these masterpieces?

Yet the complicated plot is no more difficult to build than the simple plot, involving only a little more time and labor; but the inexperienced writer usually finds the intricate plot a very unruly creature when he begins the process of elaborating it into a story. The introduction of many complications into a plot diverts the novice writer from his main course, and instead of driving steadily forward to his climax he is side-tracked from time to time and finds himself floundering in a maze of loosely connected ideas having only an indirect bearing on the plot, all of which, nevertheless, have to be drawn together into a cohesive and supple whole.

PLOTTING THE SHORT-STORY

There is always a tendency on the part of the beginner to stress unduly certain parts of even the most simple plot, and this, if carried to the extreme, is sure to play havoc with not only the balance but the movement of the story, for a story cannot move forward smoothly and confidently like a well oiled engine (as a story should move forward) if the plot is not well proportioned. This tendency to make a plot top heavy or longsided is, of course, chiefly due to the fact that the novice, having no approved methods to guide him, is forced to grope ahead blindly; but even the writer who has a knowledge of plot-anatomy, and who should therefore know better, occasionally makes the blunder of taking liberties with proportion, with the result that he creates not technically correct plots but monstrosities. Above all things, the novice should cultivate a sense of proportion, and adhere to the established rules of plot building, for it is the relative size and arrangement of the different parts that give a plot unity and sustained interest, and in these two elements is found the essence of successful plot making. Strive, too, for strength. By "strength" is meant not only a consistent and well made plot, but one fashioned out of a red-blooded idea. The writer cannot hope to build strong plots from ideas that lack vitality. Flimsy and transparent ideas afford the writer small opportunity to work up suspense during the story, and catch the reader off his guard with a smashing climax. A plot that fails to rouse the reader's interest at the very beginning and then make his interest grow up to the very end, falls far short of its purpose, and the reader who starts a story based on such a plot is apt to throw it down in disgust, the best part of it unread. The reader wants to be interested and he likes to be surprised. He enjoys matching his wits with the writer's and if he is not outwitted his contempt for the poor author is profound. You can never bore a reader with a story full of surprise-twists, but you can disappoint him and even cause him pain if your plot does not lead to an unexpected climax.

And do not forget originality! By originality I do not necessarily mean that the writer should try to unearth ideas that have never been used for plots before. Considering the fact that there are said to be only thirty-six dramatic situations, and that virtually all short stories owe their lives either directly or indirectly to one or more of these situations, this would be found a very difficult thing to do indeed. But he should try to twist the old ideas into unique forms and make combinations of single ideas new to readers. There is never a dearth of story ideas for the writer who is himself a reader (and is there any good writer who is not?). But these ideas have to be refined and recast in new molds, and it is a wise author who gives due thought and care to the process. A story with a trite or overworked plot stands little chance of finding a permanent home between the covers of a magazine, unless its fond parent is something of a genius at juggling with the king's English, and even a beautiful style of writing will not often "land" a story with a weak plot. Writers whose names are household words not infrequently have their stories rejected because of faulty plots, for nowadays editors demand something more than reputation. The magazines are always on the lookout for stories with strong, original plots, and it is the chief aim in the downtrodden author's life to give them what they want. Strive always to create, therefore; never imitate.

The *Outline for Plot Development* contains the whole theory of plot construction, and a grasp on the principles found therein is necessary to an intelligent understanding of the system of plot development that is to be elucidated in the next chapter. I have not deemed it necessary to take up each part of the plot and dwell upon it at length in this chapter, believing that the writer would be more benefited by seeing the Outline in actual use than by having it fed to him in the abstract. "A pound of fact is worth a ton of theory," some latter-day Socrates has said; and, as Mazie, our waitress once Sagely remarked, "he said a forkful." Besides, the Outline speaks in a very large measure for itself, and the writer who will take the trouble to fix its salient points in his mind will find a new interest and pleasure in the building of plots. For "placing" the germ-plot, or, more properly speaking, for identifying the most suitable field for a story-idea's growth and expansion, observe the condensed outline of a chart that follows, from which the writer may gain an idea for the preparation of a completer one for his own use:

CHART FOR PLOT CONSTRUCTION

Action: Detective, mystery, problem, fantastic, emotional, war, adventure, business, etc.

Time: Present, past or future—perhaps with specific period, as during a Peace celebration.

Setting: City, country, town, island, the sea, with specific locality.

Characters: Number: One girl and one man, etc. Occupations: Plumber, cowboy, actress, etc. Other limiting details. The characters depend, of course, a good deal on the Action, Time, Setting, Atmosphere and Mood.

Atmosphere: Humorous, joyful, sad, gruesome, religious, etc.

Mood: Good, evil, love, hate, fright, revenge, etc.

The more elaborately this chart is carried out the better. It has nothing to do with the actual structure of the plot, of course, but it plays an important part in our system of plot development, and even the casual writer will find it of inestimable value when developing plot-germs, and he may often glean an original idea from the chart itself which will start a train of thought thundering along in the right direction.

CHAPTER III - PLOT DEVELOPMENT

SIMPLE PLOT

To develop our germ-idea into a full-fledged plot or skeleton upon which to build our story, we must first analyze it carefully, use a little shrewd deduction, supply parts that are lacking, and then write the scattered parts into a lucid and logical whole. Patience, a careful survey of a story-idea; many possibilities, and a methodical summing up of the conclusions drawn from our analysis, will usually bring about the desired result.

If our mood is right and free rein is given to the imagination, it is seldom difficult to analyze a basic idea, provided it is striking or original enough to stir our sluggish minds to action; but it is sometimes hard to choose from the different fields into which our speculations are wont to lead us. The writer can rely only upon his best judgment in picking a way through the maze of possibilities that opens up before him and be guided by his individual taste.

In explaining this manner of analytic procedure, I shall confine myself at first to simple story ideas, so that the writer may get a firm grasp on the methods employed before he sets out to explore the labyrinths of the complicated plot.

By "simple story ideas" is meant embryo plots that follow the line of least resistance in unfolding. From these ideas are evolved the plots that form the basis of most short stories less than three thousand words in length. The simple plot is all that the name implies. It is usually direct in movement, and has no complications to harass the writer and distract the reader. Opening with either the inciting motive or the first incident of plot development, it marches forward over a straight road until it reaches its goal, the climax.

With a copy of the *Chart for Plot Construction* before us, let us now select a germ-plot and see exactly what we can do with it. Here is a typical plot-germ from one of my notebooks:

> *Bride and groom leave home in dead of night, bride, without wraps, groom without hat, or coat. They leave a red light burning at one of the front windows. They never return.*

What does this suggest? When we glance at the Chart there instantly leaps into mind the following: Action—mystery; Setting—city; Atmosphere—gruesome; Mood—hate. We already have our principal characters—at least, enough for the present. A title also suggests itself: "The Red Flame."

We now wish to analyze this idea, and, reading it over again, we find that these questions stare out at us:

1. Why did the bride and groom leave home in the dead of night without their wraps?
2. Why did they never return?
3. Why did they leave a red light burning at one of the front windows?
4. Where did they go?
   (a) Who saw them leave? (b) Who first saw the red light? (c) Who first entered the house? (d) What did he or she find?
5. What would be the logical outcome of the affair?

After considering the matter carefully, we might reply:

1. Because they feared some person or some thing.
2. Same answer.
3. Probably as a signal.

4.   To a foreign port, or to their death.
       (a)   Immaterial. (b) Same answer. (c) The man—or
       woman—for whom the signal was intended. (d)
       Death.
5.   The logical conclusion we draw from the foregoing is
       that when the man—or woman—who entered the house did
       not reappear within a reasonable length of time the police
       batter down the door and find the entrant lying on the floor
       dead.

This being the case, we naturally want to know:
1.   Why was the man—if it was a man—killed?
2.   The manner in which he met his death.

Reading over the analysis again, we would say:
1.   Because of the fear the bride and groom had for him;
       and as they were absent,
2.   They must have left some trap for him to walk into.

N ow, before we can draw up a working plot based on this
analysis, it will be necessary for us to select from the
material offered the four pivots around which a plot
revolves —the opening, the crisis, the crucial situation, and the
climax. The inciting motive is at once perceived in the red light the
bride and groom left burning at the window; the crisis would seem
to be the appearance of the police on the field of action; the crucial
situation when the man—or woman—enters the house; and the
climax when the police batter down the door.

Having settled upon these important points, we find it an easy
matter to fill in between them, and at once draw up a brief working
plot, using the *Outline for Plot Development* as our guide, as
follows:

THE RED FLAME

(Inciting motive): A red light is seen burning in the window of
a house and causes some comment throughout the neighborhood.
(Incident of plot development): Man declared he saw the bride and
groom who had been occupying the house leave the night before
without their wraps, as if in great haste. (First moment of
suspense): Stranger, who had been hanging around the

neighborhood for the past several days, walks up to house, peers through the window, and walks rapidly away. (Cause of crisis): Police are notified. (Crisis): They cannot enter the house, as the doors and windows are locked and barred. (Second moment of suspense): One policeman goes for an ax with which to batter down the door, the other goes around to the back of the house. (Crucial situation): Stranger returns, walks rapidly up to the house, inserts key in lock, enters house, locks and bars door after him. (Cause of climax) : A pistol shot is heard in the house and the red light goes out. (Climax): Police batter down the door. (Denouement and conclusion): Find the man lying on the floor with a bullet wound in the center of his forehead, and the following letter written in blood grasped in his hand:

> *"We saw you pass the house this evening and know that you have found us at last. You enter here thinking you will find the [whatever the author chooses], but instead you find— Death. For as you pick up this letter from the table you will release a string connected to the trigger of the gun pointed at your head, and as you die, The Red Flame dies with you."*

Seems simple enough, does it not? And it is simple, once we have a grasp on the methods to be employed. It is merely a matter of analysis and of elimination, with just enough final clearing-up of the mystery of what the stranger sought for. Of course the writer has to draw freely upon his imagination, for it takes something more than determination to make a success at the writing game. It is the technicalities of invention, generally, that bother the literary aspirant.

Let us now build up another simple plot—simple, but one that seems at first glance a little more difficult than the one we have just constructed. Suppose we select as our central idea a newspaper heading: "Girl in Wedding Gown." Stabs Self. This gives us a single crisp idea from which we are to build our plot.

Now, having let the idea percolate through our minds, we naturally want to know:

1.   Where did the girl stab herself?
2.   Why did she stab herself?
3.   When did she stab herself?
4.   What sort of weapon did she use?

Offhand we would say:

    (a)   At home, (b) in a cab, (c) or before the altar of a church during the wedding ceremony.

2.   Because she had just found out something in her intended husband's past life that promised to wreck her happiness, or (b) because she feared he would find out something in her past life which she wanted to conceal, or (c) because she was temporarily insane.

3.   On her wedding day, at some specific and significant moment.

    (a)   Stiletto, (b) hatpin, or (c) some instrument she found in the church.

Selecting the most dramatic situation from the foregoing, we find that the girl stabbed herself with a dagger before the altar because she feared the groom was about ti discover some dark deed in her past life.

So far so good, but:

1.   What did she expect the groom to find out?

2.   Why did she go as far as the church altar before carrying out her terrible design?

Her motive must have been a strong one; therefore, we are led to believe that:

1.   Perhaps she has been a Magdalene, or was already married, and

2.   She feared that her husband (as the marriage-angle seems the safer of the two possibilities) was about to reveal himself.

But, if this was the case, we are moved to ask:

1.   Why, if she already had a husband, was she about to be married again?

2.   Why did she not tell the groom her secret instead of trying to kill herself?

3.   Why did she stab herself before the altar?

Doubtless because:

1.   She had believed her husband was dead; yet

2.   Hearing that he was still living, she had, while not

believing the rumor, prepared herself for emergencies.

3.   Because she saw her husband in the congregation assembled for the wedding.

What, then, would be a logical conclusion to such a situation? Well, as the plot is a little "heavy," and we want to wind it up with the happy ending, we would say that after the bride-elect stabs herself, the groom, who had seen a man in the congregation leap to his feet in an excited manner just before the bride-to-be plunged the stiletto into her breast and rush from the church, follows the man down the street, sees him killed by a street car or in some other plausible manner, and returns to the church to find his future wife still living.

So far everything is satisfactory. But how are we going to open our working plot? If we open with the inciting motive, it will be necessary for us to do considerable preliminary skirmishing before we can get into the action of the story we have set our hearts on writing. In this case, therefore, it would seem to be advisable to skip the inciting motive and open the plot with the first incident of plot-development, and this, without a doubt, is when the bride-elect enters the church to be married. This brings us to the crisis, which would seem to be when the girl pulls the dagger from the folds of her dress. The crucial situation is found in the act of attempted self-destruction; and the climax, of course, is when the girl's lover sees the husband killed.

Based on these conclusions, we now draw up the following foundation for our story:

(First incident of plot development): Bride-elect enters church on her father's arm and walks towards the altar where the groom is waiting. (First moment of suspense): Bride suddenly turns pale and reels back. (Cause of crisis): A man in the congregation leaps to his feet and cries out. (Crisis): Girl pulls stiletto from the bosom of her dress. (Second moment of suspense): Man rushes from the church with the stifled cry "That woman is my wife!" (Crucial situation): Girl plunges dagger into her breast and falls back into the groom's arms. (Third moment of suspense): Groom utters a swift oath of vengeance and places the girl in her father's arms. (Cause of climax): Benedict-to-be rushes from the church in pursuit of husband. (Climax): Groom sees the husband run over and killed.

(Denouement and conclusion): Groom returns to find future wife, who is only slightly injured, re-reading telegram which she had received from a detective agency: "Positive proof that your husband died in South America two years ago."

There we have the plot, and by adding the telegram (probably based on mistaken identity) we not only relieve the plot of some of its "heaviness" but end it with an unexpected twist that gives the reader much food for thought.

For our next analysis, let us select a newspaper heading offering us a broader field than the one we have just developed; even though war stories are not now in demand this serves excellently as an example. The following, which seems to offer unusual possibilities, was actually clipped from a daily paper: "Convict Wins V. C.; Marries Red Cross Nurse."

After a glance at our *Chart*, we would place this plot germ as follows: Action—war; Time—during world war; Setting—depending on developments; Characters—we will start off with the one man and the girl; Atmosphere—doubtful; Mood—love.

Now, first of all we want to know something about this convict with such a unique record. Therefore, out first task is to find out:

1. Who was he?
2. Was he a soldier?
3. If so, how could a convict enlist with the army?
4. How did he win the Victoria Cross?

I t would seem very likely that:

1. He was a notorious highwayman or cracksman.
2. Yes.
3. Under an assumed name.
4. Suppose we say he saved his regiment after it had been trapped by the enemy.

Very well; but if this man was a desperado, it naturally follows that he must possess a desperado's unlovely characteristics. Therefore,

1. How could could he change his personality to such an extent that he could win the love of a refined girl?
2. Where did he meet this Red Cross nurse, and where did their romance develop?
3. How did she learn of his past (for of course she must

know his true history)?

A rather dramatic situation occurs to us. We would say that:

1.   because of a slight pressure on his brain, caused by an injury received in action, his memory up to that instant is blotted out, and because of this his whole personality has changed. (It is a fact that this has actually happened many times.)
2.   In the hospital where she nursed him through his illness.
3.   Suppose we say he revealed his past to her while delirious, following an operation to restore his memory by relieving the pressure on his brain.

All right. Now we want to know:

1.   Was the operation successful?
2.   If so, what happens?
3.   What would be a logical conclusion to the affair?

And in reply:

1.   It would be easier for us to say "no," but more interesting for us to say "yes." Therefore,
2.   After the operation the man reveals his true character to the girl, whom he fails to recognize, and she, nearly beside herself with grief, decides upon a daring course of action to save the man for herself and from himself. When he goes to sleep she places her finger over the spot on his head where the pressure has been relieved and presses it gently (the surgeon having warned her not to let anything touch this spot). And lo,
3.   When he regains consciousness it is found that the operation has been a failure, and the soldier is the same happy, cheerful, refined lover the girl has learned to love.

This analysis is fairly broad, and as the material offered seems to call for a plot of a more leisurely type than the one we last evolved, it might be well for us to open our working plot with the inciting motive. This, it appears to us, is found in the surgeon's decision to operate on the afflicted soldier.

Very good. The crisis? The operation itself. The crucial situation? When the soldier regains consciousness in the character that was his before his mind became affected. The climax, of course, is when the girl renews the pressure of that part of the unfortunate man's brain upon which the surgeon operated.

We now draw a working plot:

(Inciting motive): Soldier is informed by his sweet heart-nurse that he is to be operated on within the hour. (First incident of plot development): They discuss the matter and its many possibilities. (First moment of suspense): Surgeon says operation may fail. (Second incident of plot development): Questions soldier, bringing to light his unique record back to the time of his injury. (Cause of crisis): He is wheeled to operating room. (Crisis): Operation, the nurse assisting. (Second moment of suspense): He is brought back to his room, still under the influence of ether. (Crucial situation): He regains consciousness in his true character and, not knowing the girl, upbraids her in harsh language, and blurts out that he is a famous highwayman, of whom she has heard. (Cause of climax): The girl decides there is but one thing for her to do: the operation must be a failure. (Climax): Girl lightly presses "danger" spot on sleeping soldier's head. (Denouement and conclusion): He regains consciousness and, the operation failing because of the pressure the girl applied to his head, proves to be the tender lover she has always known.

There are great possibilities in the above plot, especially if the writer is equipped to deal authoritatively with the dual personality angle; but the author who knows little about the mechanism of the human mind would do well to side-step the psychological lead and follow some other line of reasoning in working up the plot. He would find the experiment not only interesting but instructive, and if he has his proper share of creative ability, he should be able to work out a plot which, when compared with the one we have just unfolded, would show no signs of having sprung from the same basic idea.

COMPLICATED PLOTS

The complicated plot in its development calls for a fertile imagination and a natural aptitude for mental gymnastics. It usually proves to be the despair of the writer deficient in creative ability, and even the more imaginative author sometimes finds himself hopelessly entangled in its meshes. The simple plot, as we have shown, never swerves from a straight line; the complicated plot, on the other hand, may lead us off into divers by-paths, each ending in a cul-de-sac, from which the writer has to work his way back to the main idea. The difference between the two types of plots is traceable to the basic idea. Methods of development are the same in both cases. The thing the writer has most to fear in unfolding a complicated plot is the danger of becoming lost in one or more of the many side-issues that make this type of plot what it is, and until he becomes familiar with its intricacies, he should move slowly and never let the major idea remain long out of sight. Complicated plots form the basis of most mystery and adventure stories, and in fact, the majority of other stories of more than three thousand words in length.

For our first analysis, let us take the following sentence, or rather, part of a sentence, extracted from a recent book-length portrayal of life in the West Virginia Mountains: "Melissa took the blood-oath . . . and swore to shoot Blaze on sight." A promising plot-nucleus, because it is atmospheric.

We now glance at the *Chart for Plot Construction* and choose the most suitable field for the growth of this germ-plot, which is, we believe, as follows: Action—adventure; Time—present; Setting —mountains; Characters—uncertain; Atmosphere—doubtful; Mood—doubtful, but possibly hate or revenge.

As we want our characters to be original, we at once change the girl's name to Dawn and the man's name to Jerry, and begin our probe by asking:

1. What is a blood-oath?
2. Who is Jerry?
3. Why should Dawn desire his death? Having consulted one of our mountaineer friends in regard to the first question, we promptly reply:
4. A vendetta sworn by a feudist against another feudist of a hostile clan.
5. Dawn's lover.
6. He may have betrayed her trust, or perhaps dueled with and killed one of her kinsmen.

Excellent. It appears that our principal characters are feudists and are identified with different factions. As we like to proceed plenty of with action our plots, this sounds promising. But to proceed with our inquiry:

1. Did Jerry really kill Dawn's kinsman (the duel appearing the safer of the two possibilities)?
2. If not, why has the finger of guilt been pointed at him?

After due reflection, we would say:

1. No. The slain man is Dawn's kinsman, let us say her cousin, and if our story is to have the "happy ending," it would never do for the girl's lover to be the murderer.
2. Dawn's cousin, whom we will call Boyd for the sake of convenience, has been killed by some unknown person, and relatives have accused Jerry of the murder, for they bitterly hate him because of his relations with their kinswoman.

All right. Now we want to know:

1. How and when did Dawn first hear the rumor that Jerry is guilty of the crime?
2. How did it react on her?

In reply, let us say:

1. When the dying man is brought to her cabin in the mountains.
2. As it would on any normal girl. She believes her lover to be innocent, and, having heard her kinsmen swear to avenge Boy's death, leaps upon her horse to fly to Jerry to give him warning.

A brave and noble act, and quite in keeping with the character of the average mountain girl; but we must not forget her kinsmen, who are of the same fibre that she is, and quite determined to slay Jerry as she is to save him.

Therefore:

1. Is she pursued?
2. Does she reach Jerry in time?
3. Does he protest his innocence?
4. And if the girl is followed by her kinsmen, does Jerry fight it out with them or "take to the timbers?"

After weighing the possibilities of each question, we would say:

1. She is pursued.
2. She does reach Jerry in time.
3. He does not have time to protest his innocence and leaves the girl in doubt.
4. He escapes.

Very well. Now it is necessary for us to know:

1. What becomes of Jerry?
2. Is he pursued and captured?
3. What develops?

And in reply:

1. He goes into hiding in the mountains.
2. He is pursued by the feudists, but evades them.
3. Suppose we say he hid in the mountains until nightfall and then went to the cabin of one of his kinsmen for food. He then learns, let us say, that Dawn has become convinced that he killed Boyd, after hearing two of her relatives falsely swear that they witnessed the deed, and, regretting the part she played in his—Jerry's escape, has taken the blood-oath and sworn to avenge her favorite cousin's death by shooting Jerry on sight. All of which, it should be said, is very characteristic of the untamed mountain girl.

Here we have a pretty situation and one that requires delicate handling. But, before proceeding, we should ascertain:

1. What effect did this news have on Jerry?
2. What was the result of its reaction on him?

As Jerry is a mountaineer it is very likely that:

1. He took the news calmly, and,
2. Again sought refuge in the solitudes of the mountains until he could decide upon his future course of action.

This, of course, makes it necessary for us to know:

1. What did Jerry decide to do? And,
2. What, in the meantime, has become of his pursuers?

Suppose we say:

1.   Dawn finds her lover before he reaches any decision.
2.   The pursuing feudists have lost or abandoned Jerry's trail.

Good. Dawn, bent on avenging her cousin's death, has now run Jerry to earth, and without a doubt is preparing to shoot him down. But the little vixen must never be allowed to kill the man she loves. This would be a tragedy that would ruin our chances of giving the plot a happy ending. But Dawn has shown herself to be the kind of girl no ordinary event could keep from her purpose. How, then, are we going to convince her of Jerry's innocence before she has the chance to open up with her Winchester and make a sieve out of his body? It is not likely that she would not believe anything he might say in his own defense. That is not a woman's way. Therefore:

1.   What circumstance or set of circumstances can we invent to gain the unfortunate lover an hour's respite?
2.   In the circumstances we evolve, what action does the girl take?
3.   What would be a logical conclusion to the unhappy situation?

Let us give our imaginations a chance, always keeping in mind the climax which we are now swiftly approaching.

Suppose we say that:

1.   Jerry's father (dyed-in-the-wool feudist) has been thrown from his horse and mortally injured and has asked to see Jerry before he dies.
2.   Dawn (very much a woman at heart) has promised the old feudist that she will bring Jerry to tell him good-bye before he dies if she can find him.
3.   The girl hears Jerry's father, on his death-bed, confess to his son to having killed Boyd in self-defense.

All of which is quite satisfactory. We have unearthed a ripping climax and are now ready to build our plot. We will therefore read over our analysis again and search out the inciting motive. This, without a doubt, is found in the murder of Boyd. We now look around for the crisis, and find two—the first being when Dawn flees into the night to warn Jerry of his danger, and the second, when Jerry is told that his sweetheart has sworn to kill him. The main crucial situation, of course, is when Jerry and the girl stand face to face after she has tracked him down; and the climax, when dawn overhears the death-bed confession of Jerry's father.

We now have our bearings, and by drawing freely from the facts disclosed by our analysis, draw up, without much difficulty, the following working plot:

> (Inciting motive) Wounded man is brought to dawn's cabin by kinsmen who found him dying by the roadside. (First Incident) Boyd dies in spite of all efforts to save him. (First moment of suspense) Dawn asks for information relative to the shooting. (Second incident of the plot development) Clansmen declare Boyd was murdered by Jerry. (Cause of first crisis) Feudists make preparation to hunt down Jerry. (First crisis) Dawn leaps upon her horse and, pursued by her kinsmen, begins a mad race down the mountain side to warn her lover of his danger. (Second moment of suspense) Finds him, warns him, and beseeches him to declare his innocence before they separate. (Third incident of plot development) Jerry, not having time to comply with her request because of the approach of her kinsmen, hastily kisses her, and touches only the high spots as he takes to the woods. (Cause of second crisis) Goes to kinsman's cabin. (Second crisis). He learns that Dawn has become convinced of his guilt and has sworn to "shoot him on sight." (Fourth incident of plot development) Jerry again goes into hiding. (Crucial situation). He is confronted by Dawn, who has tracked him to his hiding place. (Fifth incident of plot development) Dawn tells him his father is dying, and that she is going to grant him—Jerry—an hour's respite so he can tell the old man farewell. (Cause of climax). At the point of her rifle Dawn takes him over the mountain to his father's cabin. (Climax). The girl overhears the father on his death-bed confess to the slaying of Boyd. (Denouement and conclusion) Dawn again takes Jerry to her heart.

There we have our plot, nor did we find the building of it very difficult. This plot, which could be written into a very exciting short-story by a capable writer, is a good example of the moderate type of complicated plot.

We will now try something more complicated. The following is a condensed news item clipped from one of the daily papers.

A man is found dead in a restaurant with a beer stein in his hand and a scrap of paper lying by his body with the following words scribbled on it: 'Vile chi tradisce il segrets del confidente.'

Instantly there flashes into our mind a corking title, "The Mug of Death." With this as a "lead" we glance at our *Chart* and "place" our germ-plot as follows: Action— Detective; Time—present; Setting—city; Characters— doubtful; Mood—revenge?

Now we plunge bravely into the maze of possibilities that opens up before us:

1. How was the man killed? (a) murdered? (b) suicide? (c) natural death?
2. If he was murdered, how was it done?
3. Did his body show marks of violence?
4. Who was responsible for his death? (This, of course, depending on whether or not he was murdered).
5. Who was the victim?
6. What was in the stein?
7. What does "Vile chi tradisce il segrets del confidente" mean?
8. Who found the body and notified the police? The following answers occur to us instantly:
9. He was murdered.
10. Poison.
11. No marks of violence.
12. Murderer unknown.
13. The victim not identified.
14. Nothing in the stein.
15. Translation: "He is a coward who betrays a confidential secret."
16. The proprietor of the restaurant found the murdered man.

Before going further it might be wise to inquire:
1. What was the motive for the crime?
2. Whom do the police suspect?

And in reply:

1. The legend found by the dead man's side suggests revenge.
2. A waiter in the restaurant is suspected, though the police have no evidence upon which to arrest him.

Now, no weapons were found near the dead man, nor are there any marks of violence on his body. We have suggested that he was poisoned, but the inside of the stein was dry and therefore could have held no liquid. Some deadly gas, then. But how could gas be confined in a beer stein? Easily, by fastening down the top with a thin rim of white wax, boring a small hole in the bottom of the stein, forcing in the gas and plugging up the hole again. When the top was opened (which could easily be accomplished by a slight pressure on the edge) the victim would get a good whiff of the gas and fall back dead, while the superfluous gas escaped and left no trace of how the crime was committed.

This naturally leads us to the following questions:
1. What kind of gas was it?
2. Who was responsible for the diabolical plan?

Offhand we would say:
1. Carbon monoxide, which is one of the deadliest gases we have.
2. It must have been an "inside" job, and was doubtless "pulled off" by a waiter or the proprietor of the restaurant, who was a member of a Black Hand society. This last is suggested by the words on the scrap of paper found by the dead man's side, which are Italian.

Do the police solve this mystery? Suppose we say they do not, and that before they have completed their investigations a second man is found dead in the restaurant in exactly the same circumstances as the first victim. This gives us an opportunity to tie the plot up with a few more complications. Very well. Now, as the police have to get to the bottom of the affair, why not have a celebrated private detective undertake to unravel the mystery? If this is done, we of course want to know:
1. Did he solve the mystery?
2. If so, how?

PLOTTING THE SHORT-STORY

In reply, we would say:

1. Of course. (Fictional detectives always do!)

2. Well, suppose we say he first found out how the men were murdered, but fails to discover the murderer—although he suspects the proprietor of the restaurant whom he believes to be a famous criminal. Therefore, he plans out his course of action as follows: He will tell the proprietor confidentially that he knows who the murderer is, then order a stein of beer and see what will happen. After making the necessary arrangements with the police, therefore, he secures a duplicate of the steins used in the restaurant, conceals it in his overcoat pocket, enters the restaurant, becomes confidential with the waiter, and tells him in a loud voice so the proprietor, whom he sees standing in the kitchen door, can hear, that he is investigating the murders and that he has found out who the murderer is; then he orders beer (feeling sure, of course, that if the proprietor is the guilty man he will try to get rid of him—the detective—at once).

Well, assuming that all of this took place:

1. What happens to the detective?

2. What happens in the restaurant after the attempted murder, if there is one?

It is easy enough to see that:

1. The detective secures the stein which the proprietor (and not the waiter) brings him, and replaces it with the one in his pocket; then he falls over on the table as if dead or dying and is carried away in an ambulance.

2. The proprietor is arrested by the police and charged with the crimes.

The following questions now occur to us:

1. How did the detective make sure of his man?

2. What is a logical conclusion?

And the following answers:

(a) He finds that the stein the proprietor brought him contains carbon monoxide gas; (b) By comparing the proprietor's finger-prints (which he had secured by smearing transparent wax on a menu card) with prints in the Police Department's files and finding that he is a famous criminal who is being sought by the police of a dozen cities).

From this mass of material we now select the inciting motive, which is the discovery of the first of the two murdered men in the restaurant. A further search reveals two crises: the first, when the police declare the two dead men have evidently been the victims of the same murderer or murderers, and the second, when the detective feigns death. The crucial situation is found in the arrest of the waiter, and the climax, in the arrest of the proprietor. Therefore, after carefully reviewing our analysis, we draw up a terse working plot, as follows:

The Mug of Death

(Inciting motive) Man is found dead at a table in a small Italian wineshop. (First incident of plot development) Police declare man has evidently been murdered. (Second incident of plot development) Declare the "Vile chi tradisce il segrets del confidente" the motto of a Black Hand society. (First moment of suspense) Police investigate but fail to find clue. (Cause of first crisis) Another man found dead in the restaurant. (First crisis) Police declare that, because of the horrible expression on the man's face, they believe he died by the same hand and in the same manner as the first victim. (Third incident of plot development) Private detective undertakes to solve the mystery. (Fourth incident of plot development) Discovers how the men were murdered. (Fifth incident of plot development) Decides to trap proprietor whom he suspects, by giving him sufficient cause to wish his—the detective's—death, and an opportunity to murder him. (Sixth incident of plot development) Enters restaurant. (Cause of second crisis) Tells waiter in a loud voice he knows who the murderer is, and orders beer, which is brought to him by the proprietor, who, after depositing the stein on the table quickly leaves. (Second crisis) Detective, after securing the stein, falls over on the table as if dead. (Seventh incident of plot development) Police arrive, declare

the detective is dead, and remove the body. (Crucial situation) Waiter is arrested by the police, who still cling to their theory that he is the guilty man, and charged with the crimes. (Cause of climax) Detective returns to restaurant. (Climax) Denounces proprietor and arrests him for the murders. (Denouement and conclusion) Proprietor, believing the detective to be dead, in his fright breaks down, confesses that he was commissioned by a Black Hand society to commit the murders, and exonerates the waiter.

I n this plot we have the complicated plot at its best—or worst —as the reader prefers, for even the most ambitious author would have a hard time making it more involved than it is. As an exposition of the technic of complicated plot building, therefore, the novice should find it worthy of study. We have now covered the whole field of plot development, and nothing remains but for the writer to experiment with plots of his own. Enthusiasm is the chief requisite in plot making, and method in analytic procedure the next. Once the author has a grasp on the methods employed in plot-construction, the development of germ-ideas into technically correct working plots will not be difficult.

Chapter IV - Relations of the Plot to the Story

T he plot is the story-idea boiled down to the very essence, or, in other words, the concentrated synopsis of the story as we have evolved it in our minds and as we hope to see it materialize when we put our pens to paper to give it definite and immortal form. It has been said, and truly, that the plot bears the same relation to the story that the bony system bears to the human body.

The writer who follows our method and commits his plots to paper may at first view the result a little dubiously. The working plot is so short, so concise, that its importance is likely to be overlooked unless one has an exact understanding of the part it plays in story-writing. On first appearance, indeed, a working plot may seem to have been created for no other purpose in the world than to shackle the writer's pen and hold him down to a definite word-length. A three-thousand word story from a two-hundred word plot! Possible, of course; but what is the great idea? thinks the novice. Why waste time working up a series of threadbare ideas when the story itself is begging to be written?

These questions are soon answered when the author begins the not always easy task of writing his story. Only by experience will he learn to appreciate what it means to have a definite route mapped out for his pen to travel over when he begins to write. Experience is a hard teacher, and in the writing game it has taught us that writing a short-story without a working plot to lend us material as well as moral support is a very difficult task indeed—like eating tripe that the chef forgot to cook, for instance.

Needless to say, the working plot is not designed to cramp the author's style of writing or limit the scope of his ideas. Far from it. The function of the working plot is to keep the writer's stream of words flowing along in the right direction and makes cohesive the ideas that those words seek to express. Without a working plot—at least a mental working plot—an unwritten story is an unexplored wilderness of hazy ideas, and it is the duty of the working plot to blaze a way through that wilderness and keep the writer from wandering around in circles after he enters its confines.

Compared to the story itself, the plot of even the longest story is very brief indeed, but it is elastic and subject to different degrees of expansion. The word-length of a story to be written around a given plot depends entirely upon the author. Some writers have a diffusive style of writing, others are very sparing of their words; and an author is sure to adhere to his own particular style when he begins the process of elaborating a plot into a story. Give two writers the same plot and the chances are they will produce stories varying many hundreds of words in length.

Although we have at this time no intention of entering the sacred precincts of story-writing, except in its relation to the plot, the word-length of stories falls, we believe, well with in our sphere of consideration, and having touched this important subject it might be well to comment further upon it. The modern short story calls for speed and snap. We have made this remark before, but, if one is to judge by the number of spineless manuscripts that swell the average editor's daily mail, it will bear repetition many times. The story must be placed before the reader with delicate though trip-hammer strokes. Readers who seek mental relaxation in short-stories are usually busy people who read in much the same manner that they eat–quick-lunch style. They have not the time to wade through pages of rambling descriptive matter or absorb weighty paragraphs of philosophic reflection. They refuse to be instructed; they want to be amused, and like their stories served up piping hot, as it were.

In writing the short story, therefore, the author should be succinct, but never, of course, to the point of sacrificing clearness. If his style of writing is diffusive, he should either try to cultivate a more direct and pointed style or turn to one of the literary forms offering a wider range for expression than the short-story. With some exceptions, of course, short stories by novelists are apt to bore the reader to the point of distraction. The reason is that most novelists have a diffusive style of writing, and verbiage is out of place in the shorter fictional forms. The beginner should not ignore this fact. It is one of the secrets of successful short-story authorship that has cost many a writer dearly to learn. "Brevity is the life of the short-story," O. Henry said, and he knew whereof he spoke.

The short story should not be confused with the novelette. At the very outside, the short-story is limited to eight thousand words, while the novelette may run up to twenty-five or thirty thousand words. If the first draft of a story runs over the prescribed number of words, as it often will, the writer should steel his heart and wade in with the pruning shears.

Most experienced authors revise their stories several times before they submit them to magazines, and consider that they have done a good day's work when they succeed in cutting a five-thousand-word story, say, down to three thousand words or less. Revising a manuscript is a heart-rending task until the writer learns to look at his work from an impersonal and critical standpoint. It is hard to rip out beautifully formed sentences and paragraphs one has labored and sweated over, but at times very necessary; and the writer may expect no mercy from the unfortunate editors upon whom he inflicts his manuscripts until he learns to weigh word-values accurately and impartially. There are, of course, a few magazines that publish nine and ten-thousand word stories which they are pleased to term short, but an analysis of these stories will show that most of them are either novelettes or very verbose short stories which only the exalted names of authors succeeded in "putting over."

It will be seen, therefore, that while the working plot itself places no restriction on the word length of a story, the writer should always endeavor to keep himself within the established bounds; nor should he ever leave the word length of a story to chance. The author should study the plot and come to some decision in regard to the matter before the story is begun. This calls for good judgment. Each part of the plot must be weighed separately, because the word-lengths of the different parts vary. It is simply a matter of values that can be learned only by experience. The most finely proportioned plot can be made into a very lopsided story by a careless writer. Proportion in story-writing, be it said, is as essential as it is in plot building.

In trying to determine the proper word-length of a story to be written, the author should first size up the plot as a whole and decide what is, in his opinion, the least number of words it will take for him to write it into an interesting and convincing story. He should then try to determine the proportionate value of each part of the plot and estimate the number of words it will take to give it expression. If his judgment is frequently in error, let him not be dismayed. Even the trained writer cannot always sense the proportionate values of the different parts of a plot before he begins to write, but when he gets the story in rough draft he is able to see the plot in perspective, so to speak, and can then judge the importance of each part accurately. This applies to the beginner as well as to the old-timer. All this means that the writer must expect to revise, and revise, and revise. Then, after he has done his best, he can only commit his story to the mails and leave the rest to Fate—and the editors.

In casting about for a story to illustrate the relation of the plot to the story, two considerations have guided us in making a selection; first, the limits of the space allotted to us in the pages of this magazine, and second, our desire to select a story that would clearly illustrate the point we wish to make. The story we have chosen is tersely told and the plot is very simple; it is therefore, we believe, well suited to our purpose. The story was first published in the New York Sun several years ago, and is reprinted here by permission of the editors of that paper.

The plot for this story was worked out by the methods described in our previous articles. The germ-plot from which it was developed was a one-line newspaper heading: "Man Steals To Keep Wife From Starving." We have not deemed it necessary to give here our analysis of this basic idea, as the process for developing a plot-germ into a working plot has already been fully explained; but we have introduced a copy of the plot we evolved from the idea in order that the writer may follow us step by step over the gradual course of its elaboration into a short-story.

The writer should make a study of this working plot be fore he tackles the story itself, and either memorize it or refer to it from time to time during his perusal of the literary effort in its completer form. We make this suggestion be cause we are anxious for the literary aspirant to see exactly how each separate part of the plot was built up in the story, and how the several sections were joined together. Only in this way can he hope to arrive at a fair estimate of the value of each part of the plot and gauge the relative importance of the word-groups connecting the different sections; and he must be able to do this if he desires to understand the part each section plays in giving the story unity and proportion.

Later on the novice would do well to write a story of his own around the plot, and compare it with the version that appears below. If the result is satisfactory, he can then begin the building of new plots with confidence. The story as we have written it contains approximately one thousand words. The writer should strive to keep his version of the story within this word-limit, and then see if he can, in his own Opinion, improve upon it by increasing the Word length to sixteen or eighteen hundred words. If convenient, he should then get some disinterested "literary sharp" to read the several versions and comment upon them, for criticism, when it is sincere and constructive, is one of the young writer's most valuable assets. Even the most hardened free-lance welcomes it because it fattens his bank account, and this, be it known, he considers the sweetest and most beautiful thing in the world.

WORKING PLOT

> *(First incident of plot development) A man stages a high way robbery in order to procure money to buy food and medicine for his ill wife. (First moment of suspense) He holds up a pedestrian. (Cause of crisis) With the money he took from his victim he buys food and hurries home. (Crisis)*

99

He finds his wife dead. (Second incident of plot development) Believing that Gos deprived him of his wife to punish him for the sin he committed, he resolves to wash the sin from his soul by reimbursing the man he robbed. (Second moment of suspense) Having, after many hardships, accumulated sufficient money to do this, he sets out to find the victim of the hold-up. (Crucil situation) His untiring efforts are at last rewarded and he locates the man for whom he has been searching. (Cause of climax) He steps forward to make amends. (Climax) The man proves to be a detective and places our erring hero under arrest. (Denouement and conclusion) The detective tells him the money he stole was counterfeit.

There is one very important point in the foregoing plot to which we desire to direct the writer's attention before he takes up the story that follows. It is the *opening*. It will at once be perceived that the inciting motive of this plot is the necessity that drives the man to crime. But as our story was to be very short, we wanted to jump at once into the action of it, and avoided opening the plot with the inciting motive, which would have called for at least one introductory paragraph, by starting off with the first incident of plot development and explaining in the very middle of it what the story was all about. And this, as we remarked in one of our previous articles, is always a good plan to follow when the story idea is flexible enough to permit of it.

God's Will.

First incident of plot development.

Joshua waited, crouched behind the clump of shrubs, until the man was directly opposite him. Even then his courage almost failed him; but he suddenly remembered the wife who lay in the cold, bare room at home, dying dying for the want of proper food to nourish her poor emaciated body, and without further hesitation he sprang out on the sidewalk and thrust his unloaded revolver in the man's face.

First moment of suspense.

"Hands up!" he said, huskily.

The man stopped, laughed, and elevated his hands.

"A hold up?" he said genially.

Joshua nodded.

Descriptive: The robbery.

"I am sorry to-inconvenience you," he stammered, as he slipped his hand in the man's pocket and drew forth a roll of bills. "But— but my wife—I will only take a little."

"Oh, help yourself," said the other, looking at Joshua curiously. "A new hand at the game, eh?" he added.

"My first offense."

"Well, let it be your last," said the man dryly. "Your hand is too unsteady for this kind of work."

Joshua selected ten ten dollar bills from the roll of greenbacks and thrust the rest back into the man's pocket.

"Thank you," he said wearily, "and goodnight."

Anticipatory: Suggesting reflex of developments.

"Au revoir," said the man with a queer laugh, "but not goodnight."

Cause of crisis.

As he turned the corner and disappeared in the gloom,

Joshua threw his useless revolver from him and made his way rapidly down the street, the hundred dollars clutched tightly between his numb fingers. At the corner grocery he paused long enough to purchase a plentiful supply of dainties for Mary, and then hurried on through the cold streets to her bedside.

Crisis.

When he reached home his wife was dead.

Explanatory: Showing how the crisis reacted on the principal character.

"It is God's will," he whispered as he knelt by the bedside. "This is my punishment for the great wrong I have done this night. But I will right myself in the eyes of God and Mary. This, too, is God's will, and God's will be done."

Descriptive: Aftermath of crisis.

On the following day Joshua buried what remained of the woman he loved, using the rest of the hundred dollars to give her a decent burial. After the funeral he did not return to his home. He felt that he could never again enter the room where he had knelt on the bare floor by the side of his wife through that long night of anguish. Mary was dead now; home was a thing of the past.

Second incident of plot development.

So he turned his face toward the city and started out in search of work. For he now had but one purpose in life, and that was to earn one hundred dollars by the sweat of his brow to reimburse the man he had robbed. For this was the Great Sin, he thought, that he must wash from his soul before he was ready to stand in the presence of God and Mary.

Descriptive: Paving the way to the second moment of suspense.

> *Throughout the winter Joshua toiled at what odd jobs he could pick up, for work was scarce and his unkempt appearance barred him many doors that might otherwise have been opened to him. But he found work of a kind, and though he was but poorly paid, he thanked God for each copper he dropped into the dirty tobacco bag he carried pinned under his shirt, smiling bravely the while at the hunger that often pinched his cheeks and the cold gusts of wind that whistled through his threadbare clothes. For in thought he found much of his food, and the eyes of Mary, which ever smiled down upon him, gave him warmth.*

Second moment of suspense.

> *At las arrived the great day when Joshua had accumulated one hundred dollars, and he set himself the task of finding the man he had wronged. He did not know exactly how to go about it; but he set forth trustingly, confident that his reward would come to him in due time.*

Descriptive: Showing the difficulties Joshua encountered in the second phase of his task.

> *Day after day he patrolled the streets scanning the faces of the passing throng. His unkempt figure soon became familiar in ally and on boulevard alike, and as he limped by on his tireless way many a man and woman gazed into his pinched face and wondered at the expression they found stamped thereon.*

Descriptive: Leading up to the crucial situation.

> *The days passed and winter merged into spring, and still Joshua marched on toward his goal. The bleak days and nights had used him hardly; his clothes were rags; his shoes hung to his feet by shreds; his cheeks were hollow; his eyes*

glazed; but his determination was as firm as on the day he had started out on his quest, and if he at times faltered as he limped about town, it was because of weakness of body and not from instability of purpose.

Crucial situation.

And then one day he found The Man. The instant Joshua saw him as he came out of a little cigar store, he knew his quest was ended. For he could never forget the face of the man he had wronged; it had been stamped on his brain by the weight of anguish.

For an instant he was so overcome by joy that he could not move or speak; then he stepped quickly forward and touched The Man on his arm.

Cause of climax.

"One moment, please," he said huskily.

The Man stopped and looked at him sharply, "Well?"

Joshua cleared his throat.

"Months ago," he said, "I wronged you—"

Climax

"Ah, I remember you," said The Man quickly. "I am a detective and I never forget a man's face." He dropped his hand on Joshua's shoulder. "You are under arrest for highway robbery."

Opening the way for the denouement and conclusion.

Joshua smiled happily.

"That is God's will," he said, "and I will go with you gladly. But first let me return the hundred dollars—"

Denouement and conclusion.

"Oh, that," said The Man with a laugh. "Forget it. The bill was a counterfeit."

CHAPTER V - BONUS PLOT-GERMS

Editor's note: okay, so this chapter did not come from the same source as the preceding article series. The same author (Culpeper Chunn) wrote it for the November, 1916 issue of "The Writer." I thought it felt right at home with this series, though, and so I have included it. It may very well be useful as you start up your own plot-germ notebook.

- A noted surgeon is performing a difficult operation on a wealthy patient at night. The light goes out, the surgeon loses his nerve and drops the scalpel; the nurse catches it and as the light comes on she plunges the knife into the surgeon's heart. Why did she kill the surgeon? Why at such a critical moment? Did she complete the operation herself?
- A man finds a broken cane on the street he discovers that the handle conceals a small blood covered dagger. A white faced girl runs up to him gasps out, "89," and falls dead at his feet.
- Two famous detectives suspect each other of having committed a certain crime and try to fasten the guilt on each other!
- Strange sounds are heard coming from an unoccupied house — two adventurous girls go in to investigate and never return. What caused the noise? What became of the girls?
- A girl in male attire is found dead. Where was she found? Why and by whom was she killed? Why was she in male attire?
- A doctor returning home late at night after receiving a mysterious telephone call to attend a patient, finds a strange dead man lying on the floor of his library.

- A cowboy adopts a baby he finds abandoned at a water hole. Does he find later that it is the child of the girl he loved and lost? If so what happens?
- An advertisement appears in a paper "Wanted a girl who is not afraid of anything." What is the job? What happens to the girl who gets it?
- A nurse in a hospital finds a picture of her missing lover on the body of an unidentified girl who has been killed in an automobile accident. On the back of the picture are the numbers "813."
- A man falls in love with the photograph of a girl he finds on the street. He discovers after he has fretted himself to the verge of a nervous breakdown and the detectives have declared they cannot find the original of the photograph, that the picture is of his wife and was taken before he was married.

Here is the general process for plotting the short story.

Keep a notebook of plot germs/ideas.

When you decide on an idea to use, as it a bunch of questions: why? who? where? what happens next? etc. As you start to get an idea, write down meta information about the story, including:

- Genre
- Time
- Setting
- Characters
- Atmosphere
- Mood

This is what the article calls the Chart for Plot Construction.

Once you have the chart, start mapping out the point to the general plot outline.

1. Incident of plot development.
2. First moment of suspense.
3. Cause of crisis.
4. Crisis.
5. Second moment of suspense.
6. Crucial situation.
7. Cause of climax.
8. Climax.

How to Write a Fight Sequence

By Robert J. Hogan

From 1954 Writers Yearbook

The most elementary fight is the single-blow affair. The hero socks the villain, knocks him down and the fight is over. Since the action is so very brief, there is no suspense unless we have had a prolonged build-up to this fight. There is little reader satisfaction in the one-punch action.

Ever watch your professional fights on television? Analyze those fights to learn what it was in one fight that pleased you.

The same principles apply to fiction fight sequences. Recall the groans of sport writers and the public after a one-sided championship fight. The contestants were supposed to be evenly matched. The fight was a sellout. The publicity build-up had been terrific. The time for the fight arrived. Joey Doakski steps up and catches the champ with a beaut. And the knockout occurs in one minute and fifty-three seconds of the first round. There is a wasted evening.

Take the other kind of fight; more often you'll find this in the less-publicized affairs. One fighter knocks the other down, the downed man gets up at the count of nine and knocks the other out but the bell saves him. Both boys pant in their corners waiting to get back at it. But now they are cautious. We see some very fancy ducking and weaving and playing for time. No waltzing or stalling or clinching but feeling each other out, hunting for that weakness. Close to the end of the second round they both open up. What you hoped was coming lands, and there you are, satisfaction all over the place as one sags. But he catches himself and in wild desperation fights back and we end that round in a frantic slugging match. So it goes for ten or fifteen rounds or maybe only six. And remember six rounds of that sort of thing is an eternity if you're in the ring. But there is a fight.

That is the kind of a fight a reader likes, whether it is a fight between women in a barroom brawl, boarding-school girls fighting in a dark dormitory bedroom, a pair of Pier 64 brawlers or two stallions fighting it out to the death.

The length of time or words to let a fiction fight run, should be gauged by the length of the story, the importance of the fight scene to the story and how long the reader can be held.

Generally speaking, one fight of two pages in a short story would be plenty. A 60,000-word novel may have two, three or even four fights and one of the fight could be as much as a seven- or eight page chapter in length.

We may have the hero against one, two-or half a dozen villains, as in the picture Shane–and still make it fairly convincing.

If the writer has had ring experience he should watch for professional-sounding terms in back-country brawls. He must not have a wild-swinging bruiser from a lumber camp slipping, countering, ducking and acting like a pro. The lumberjack must flail away with haymakers. If a hero or villain is fairly skillful at the art, it is natural for him to do some ducking, left leading and uppercutting. Tie your terms to the fighter and see that they fit.

There was a fight between two women a while back that came off rather well. A high-spirited fighting spinster who could split an ear of her lead mules with a lap line or a bullwhip, met a gal from the town gambling house. The gambling house gal rode a horse and was armed only with a riding crop, or quirt. As long as the spinster could work at some distance with her bullwhip, she did very well. But the gambler gal rode in close, tried to run down and trample the spinster with her horse, meanwhile beating at her with her quirt. The spinster was in a bad way until she pulled down the lash of her bullwhip and doubled it for a club. The fight turned into quite a battle as she beat the fighting horse and the girl rider with the clubbed whip, while the horse tried to knock her down by striking hoofs and the quirt cut up her face. Altogether, it had the ingredients of a good fight, each gal, as she was about to lose, finding some additional help in clubbed bullwhip, striking hoofs, etc. Back and forth the battle surges, makes it suspenseful.

But keep the chances almost even, giving the villain the edge until the end. If the hero is winning too easily, let an enemy drop out of a tree, jump from the end of her bar, swing from a chandelier and down him. When the hero is about to be finished, he rises with the last ounce of that stuff called courage and beats his way back to semi-victory. This victory must not come, however, until the very end and never easily. Winning, the hero walks away, bruised and bleeding; straight and brave, with a slight swagger, maybe to fall on his face from exhaustion, outside, where nobody can see him. Remember the knife fight in the movie "From Here to Eternity." Pruitt kills the stockade officer and then falls in exhaustion on the threshold of his girl's house.

The villain may be as dirty as he likes. The hero, no. Don't make the hero a saint who stands in the appropriate pose and fights like a gentleman. Let him throw some chairs and do a good job of brawling, as long as the villain does worse. When the hero is down he may use wrestling tactics and throw the villain off balance and such. He may even break the villain's arm, but never can he kick the villain in the groin. That's a little low for the hero no matter what.

Plausibility is important, but the term, literary license, applies to a fight sequence as well as to any other part of the story, and, by going a little beyond the probable you'll have a more thrilling fight. Let the hero—or villain-accomplish some almost impossible act. When the hero is down on his back and all but out and the brutal boot of the villain is about to crush his skull, it is possible for the hero barely to manage to duck the boot and catch it with both hands. A wrestler or one skilled in judo could throw the kicker on his ear by a hard twist of foot and leg, although the average fighter would not be able to. It furnishes a shift of events and allows your hero to rise and fight again.

Be sparing of that sort of power. Don't make either the hero or villain a superman. In re-writing, check for repetition. Don't say, "He *punched* him in the nose, let drive a right *punch* to the jaw, *counter-punched* his left eye." Some of the talented word men of radio and TV repeat themselves horribly in the excitement of battle.

Starting the fight is fairly simple but here again appeal to the reader's love of the underdog. If possible, let the hero get socked first. In a gun fight, let the hero be surprised with little chance to draw.

When the fight is started, the hero may, if he is the more clever of the two, begin at once to outguess the villain. Perhaps he plays for time, acting almost like a coward at first, keeping away from the enemy until he can taunt him. He may have found at the opening that the villain fights blindly if sufficiently angered. From here on, the movement is studied, each punch is pictured, the missing, the landing and the result. The hero does well enough in the first flurry after being clipped when he had no reason to expect the attack. He beats the villain back, might even let up a little for the moment. But the villain comes in wild, and his unorthodox style lets the villain slip by two good rights of the hero and land a Sunday right that spins the hero and smacks him into a corner. Now the hero manages to get up before being trampled, only to learn that the villain has friends. The hero spins a chair in the way of one and takes on the other. But he finds a third fighting on the villain's side.

The hero doesn't have to win. You may produce an unusual story if the hero loses.

Behind all fighting there must be a reason. Long past are the days when a writer could push a stranger into a bar and have a big lug sock him because he didn't like his looks. If you want to sell the story, there must be a darn good reason why they fight. Not just name calling but a world of basic enmity behind it all. In the story, Shane, the hero had a deep-laid reason why he finally went after Wilson. The reason went deeper than the immediate excuse for the fight itself. It was the old force of good vs. the force of evil. The Saviour downing the devil.

The finish of a fight can well be the most dramatic and suspenseful scene in the entire story. Take the screen version of "Stage Coach." John Wayne and the villain brothers have fought it out in the dark of the deserted main street. We leave John Wayne lying in the street, likewise a villain brother or two. The scene switches to the inside of the bar. We see every man in the saloon, eyes popping, staring at the one villain brother who half staggers, half reels into the bar, alone. It is an almost sure sign that John Wayne is dead, that the bad is victorious. The brother reaches for the bar, misses, reels slightly, and falls flat on his face and lies there in the sawdust. We know that John Wayne has won after all. That one brief scene is a moment of high art in the picture-making industry. So let it be with story writing.

I don't know about you, but I totally want to know what was the context of the gambling house girl vs spinster fight example.

All in all, I think there's a lot of good things to consider in this article, with one thing that really stuck out to me: "*Behind all fighting there must be a reason.*" Two people slugging it out can be very boring if the fight doesn't mean anything. If you define very clearly the characters' motivations, or at least their goals, chances are the reader will identify with one or the other and become emotionally invested.

LET YOURSELF GO

by James H. S. Moynahan

From the October, 1940 issue of Writer's Digest.

Roger Torrey, who does the Marge and McCarthy series in Black Mask, stopped over at the house one Sunday afternoon with Helen Ahern, and I asked Helen how she was doing on a story she'd been working on.

Roger winked at me. "She's holding her own," he said, mock-loyally. "She's still on page 26!"

Helen joined in the general laughter. She knew the *we* all knew, too.

The casual quip started me thinking. Why do we strike those impasses, and what gets us out of them?

I've come to the conclusion that one of the most important factors is this: We stall because we don't *feel* our story. We have a few rough ideas, but no strong emotional reaction to them.

Steve Fisher, whose stuff you have read in Liberty, Cosmo, and will read shortly in the Post, puts plenty of study into this business of what makes a yarn tick. After I saw the Dorothy Lamour picture *Typhoon,* which carries story credit in big letters on the screen for Steve, I asked him what, in his opinion, did he consider the most important factor in selling his stories.

"That's easy," he said. "Mood is easily the most important essential. Back in the days when I was writing pulp, I used to fly in the face of editorial tradition in a lot of offices by turning in stories that had a strong emotional pitch running through them. You had to write action to sell, of course, but I always tried to include that other element, an emotional tone that held throughout the story. Hit that and hold it, and your story writes itself."

The story we had been reading and discussing was a mood-picture of the war in France, held together by a mounting sense of impending tragedy that reaches its peak in battle and hospital scenes. In these it was not difficult to feel the impact of the writer's emotional reaction to his material.

He didn't just report them mechanically; he threw himself into the soldier's stat of mind; his desperation, his fury, his resignation, his despair.

Such writing calls for telling in the first person, as you would set down your feelings in a letter to a friend. In a third person story the same emotional writing would seem forced and patronizing, as if the reader were too stupid to gather what the hero's emotions must have been from the recital of the events themselves.

So there you have it. Unless, that is, you think Steve doesn't know himself why he sells!

For my part, I think he's got something. I'd like to go a little further with it, though.

I'd like to see whether we can't examine this business of mood, and discover *just* how to evoke it in the reader. Steve feels it–and he writes it as he feels it. I think you've got to do that, ultimately, but maybe there are some steps that precede the writing. Let's see what *does* move people,

I'm not going to be chump enough to try and get you dabbing at your eyes over bits lifted from stories. So, even if you weep at card tricks, l don't think I'm letting you in for any emotional orgy. What I hope to do is illustrate a principle, and show you how you can use it to lift the pitch of your own yarns, This excerpt's from *The Blue Light*, Private Detective, August, 1939, by Henri St. Maur. The detective, Fort, has just phoned his client that the murder mystery has been cleaned up.

> *He hung up, turned to Judy, (His office assistant) "Well, sweet, that's how it is. Now if you'll tell me what Stoughton did with the pistol-the little twenty-five he had when you conked him this morning-we'll have him sewed up."*

> *Judy started at him. "I conked him?"*

> *Fort said impatiently: "Stop it. Stop it! Are you asking me to believe that a timid kid like this Armitage girl wouldn't*

run for her life if she saw Stoughton in my office? No, what happened, darling, was that you saw him going for her, and you conked him. It wasn't till after he'd worked on you with that Tyrone Power act of his that you fell, What'd he do-promise you a cut on the take if you planted the card on my desk?"

Judy's lips peeled back from her teeth and she clawed the little gun out from the bosom of her dress. Fort jumped at her, slapped the gun down.

"Don't make it worse, you little fool!" he said. His voice held only bitterness. He twisted the gun from her singers, put it in his pocket.

"Get out of here," he said in a low, controlled voice. "Get out of here."

The girl looked pitifully at him, "Oh, Al, I-"

"Get out," he said between his teeth.

She looked at him, lowered her eyes, went through the door.

Fort, blood dripping from his slashed arm, watched her take her hat and coat from the rack, go out without looking back.

Behind him the Armitage girl said: "Oh, Mr. Fort, do you suppose they'll get my things back?"

Fort said, not looking around: "Maybe." His lips were shut white. His fists were knots.

She said: "Maybe you could work on it for me."

Fort didn't turn. "Maybe I could," he said slowly. "Maybe I could."

I n Roger Torrey's *Party Murder*, Black Mask, April, 1934, a
police Captain has just learned of the death of his daughter.
Dal Prentice is the hero, a lieutenant of detectives. He is
phoning.

> *He could hear somebody say say: "Hold it!" then: "You,
> Dal?"*
>
> *"Uh-huh!"*
>
> *"Dal! They just picked up the... what's left of my girl off
> Aldena Boulevard. She's been dumped out of a car."*
>
> *"Oh... my... good... lord!"*
>
> *"Dal! Doc says her head was just beaten in. Let that go and
> come down."*

After some discussion, Prentice hangs up.

> *The phone clicked and Prentice turned a somber face to his
> audience, (His two partners and a prisoner).*
>
> *"Cap's feeling bad, They found his girl for him."*
>
> *Peterson (one of the police detectives) said: "I've got two and
> I could hear what was said..."*

L et's start with these two illustrations. Can you see what they
have in common? Can you see how, in the complete story
they might tend to evoke emotion in the reader? And why?
The explanation for the reader's emotional reaction is this:
empathy-or, if you prefer, sympathy.

Have you over wondered why mob will react so violently to
things that its members, as individuals, might very well ignore? Or
why a comedy is funnier in a full house? Or why you can read a
headline: *Thousand Chinese Slaughtered in Battle*, with dry eyes,
and yet weep over a dead puppy of your own daughter's?

The answer is sympathy. Emotion is catching. A loud, angry,

furious voice makes us irritable even if it is not addressed to us at all. Its mere sound evokes anger in us.

Thus, in the examples above, we take our cue from the characters' emotional reactions. Had the writers made the characters meet these emotional crises with indifference, we ourselves should not be moved, but should find ourselves meeting the challenge of the situation with the same emotional indifference.

For example, in the first excerpt, substitute for words like "bitterness" words like "amusement," "boredom," "indifference." Watch what happens to the emotional tone.

For: "His lips were shut white. His fists were knots," substitute: "He glanced down idly at his nails. They were clean and symmetrical."

High spot in the Torrey excerpt is the point where Peterson says: "I've got two and I could hear what was said..." Just as Peterson, himself a father, is quick to respond with ready sympathy to the news of his chief's tragedy, so the spectacle of a fellow human being responding thus to a situation tends to make us automatically respond *in the same fashion*. And note here that we might have responded with anger, with indignation, with despair, with indifference, or any number of shades of emotional reaction. Later in the story, when other characters become angered over developments, we find our own pulse rising, too.

Now the point, for you, is this. If you write a beautiful scene, full of menace, terror, and fury, and in it you show no character reacting to these stimuli *as you wish have your reader react,* what do you do now?

You take the yarn out, and carefully write in passages showing how the characters react to your menace. And remember: The more moved they are by story developments, the more moved your reader is going to be. Up to a point.

That point is incredibility. If you go too far-if you have your heroine throwing a wing-ding at his frown, like Sweet Alice, Ben Bolt, then you must expect your reader to say: "Sa-a-ay! What is this! Take it *easy,* will you!"

The trick is to force the emotion, to make your characters react as violently as possible or as deeply as possible to a given situation, but only up to a point which is still logical, and credible. Overdo it, and your drama will spill over into laughs.

Now not all this depicting of your characters reacting

emotionally will be done by saying to the reader in so many words: "My hero is gritting his teeth. He's biting his lips." I think some of the biggest kicks a writer gets out of his trade is working out more subtle ways of showing these reactions without describing them in so many words.

For example, the way Fort, in the first excerpt, reiterates: "Get out of here." We don't say he's obsessed with that single idea, but can it be done more effectively? We could tell the reader that the Armitage girl is a silly, self-centered little fool who misses entirely the significance of what his secretary's treachery means to Fort. But her insensibility, so necessary here for *contrast,* is brought out in her complete preoccupation with her own lousy little "things."

Note, in the Torrey excerpt, that the reader is not beaten over the head with adjectives, the distracted father is only a voice, yet we sense his controlled agony better than if we were having it described to us. You can do a lot just with the use of a person's first name, as you see here. And note the grimness of Peterson's "I've got two, and I could hear what was said." We can just see this big, human cop holding back his feelings and resolving to handle this murder as if it had been one of his own two kids that had been the victim.

Instead of cluttering up your next yarn with long descriptions of your characters' emotional throes, try seeing how much you can do with dialogue alone. Try figuring out how many devices you can hit upon to do the work instead. For example:

"B-but I can't g-go in th-there! Do you want me to be k-killed!"

"John. Please, now, John! He's just a *child.* John, ple-e-ase!"

"Will you shut up!"

"I... see. A *wise* guy, huh?"

"Why you, you... !"

And so on. Repetition, stammering and stuttering, meaningful pauses, despairing wails, little intimate, impulsive appeals-give dialogue first chance at delineating these.

Where you do find the need for pantomime, use it as sparingly as possible. That is to say: One good effect is worth ten mediocre ones. For economy of effect, James M. Cain's *The Postman. Always Rings Twice* will well repay any study you may give it. You will find numberless effects such as the part where the new helper, finding himself alone with the Greek's wife, locks the door and comes inside carrying a plate and fork as an excuse to make conversation. When he says: "The fork on the plate was rattling like a tambourine," he's told you everything.

One more thing. Rules for writing are never of much use until their employment has become second nature and you no longer think consciously about them. Don't expect these suggestions to help you right away. They may even confuse you and upset your writing for a while.

But here's one rule for evoking emotion I *can* give you that you can put to work right away, and one that won't give you any trouble. It's this:

Let yourself go. When you're writing about emotion, throw yourself into the feeling you want the character to experience, and write out of your own emotion. If you can do that, then everything I've told you above is just the malarkey, because you'll do it *instinctively* so much better that any rules, no matter how effective, must necessarily step aside for reality. Because that's what you'll be writing.

Your readers will feel something while reading your work. You don't want it to be boredom. So give them a protagonist to relate to with big emotions.

How to Revise a Novel

By Carol Kendall

Originally published in April 1946 issue of Writers Digest.

T hey're rewritten.
Especially detective novels.
If I were the sort of person who needs to stare a Good Thought in the eye every morning, that is the slogan I would hang over my typewriter.

Rewriting is the fourth R in my business. Until Harper and Brothers took an interest in "*The Black Seven*," though, I rather innocently supposed that an author wrote, he submitted, and if he were lucky, he sold with some slight further revisions. Perhaps some writers do work that way, but I'll wager they're not beginners. And I'm talking about the beginner, the person who has never sold a novel, the little gent with the gleam in his eye who strews paper like milkweed about the room. He writes, he sometimes revises. And then-if he is wise and wants to get out of the category of beginner–he rewrites.

But let us take the case of you. You are an intelligent person who knows about typing manuscripts on one side of the paper only. You have a flair for writing and a tenacity of purpose. You have a good idea for a detective novel and, after conscientiously mapping out the plot in detail you know just when the second body falls out of the closet on Sally Fingerhut, who is getting out her golf clubs even though it is the dead of winter (a suspicious circumstance), you complete a rough draft of the entire novel. If you stop at this point–and happen to be a genius, you may sell the novel. If you are not a genius, the chances are that your ms. will remain a ms.

You must now revise. On page 6 the newspaper publisher's

name appears as Cyrus and on page 60 he is called Cyril. You discover that John Aubrey, the District Attorney, barks, growls, snarls, spits, grumbles, snorts, bays and bellows, a progression of sounds more in keeping with a hound than with a public official.

This revision is fun. You change a word here, add a sentence there, reword a paragraph, and lo, the novel is finished. You picture the fortunate editor who is about to be the recipient of your book. He is sitting in his office sunk in a veritable Slough of Despond because he needs a good detective novel for his lists and all his old writers are either taking the cure or having babies. So you type out your novel on clean white paper. You place it lovingly in a box...

Stop right there. If you're really in earnest about this novel, don't send it off now. Put it in your bottom bureau drawer (under your out-of-season sweaters where you won't run across it by accident) and leave it. Leave it for at least six weeks. Six months would be better, but if your will power is no stronger than mine, six weeks must suffice for aging.

At the end of this time haul out the novel. Make yourself as comfortable as possible because the ordeal is going to be rough. Don't fill up on doughnuts for breakfast. I would advise something ascetic like grapenuts or all-bran and coffee. Your intellect must be purged and pure.

The first page will seem pretty good to you. Opens well, you mutter into your coffee. You let your backbone take on the curve of the chair. Lordy, that's pretty good, you say on page 5. I don't remember writing that sentence at all. You read on. Then, while you, are sitting there all defenseless with your cooling coffee and your cigarette, it happens. That humorous scene between John Aubrey and Terry Williams, your private investigator, makes a great pancake right before your eyes. It is followed by another and flatter pancake when Ellen Russet is "grilled" (you wince at the word) by the redfaced and unlettered Sergeant Bundy. Ah, but here comes that touching moment when Terry defends Ellen because of her green eyes. You *know* this scene is a knockout.

You read it. Your face, begins to burn. You creep to the kitchen for a fresh cup of coffee. The blinding light has flashed into the very crannies of your brain. Your private investigator, your hero, Terry Williams, is an absolute ass. Besides being an ass, he is a prig, a driveler and a dolt. On second thought you'll make that two cups of coffee, and with renewed strength you want to tear up the manuscript and feed it to the fire.

Don't do it. Burn up the impulse instead. You are now in a healthy frame of mind to continue. Nothing escapes your gloomy eye. You discover that the clue of the long cigarette butt is childish and unconvincing. The love affair between Terry and Ellen stagnates, and Terry, besides being all the aforementioned things, is a monumental bore. The murder of Cyrus Weston is lacking in motivation; the murder of Carleton March is pure ostentation.

The Dean of Women at my university had a panacea for that moment when you just can't stand it any longer: take a long, long walk. I don't believe it was the writing urge she had in mind, but the advice is sound. You must now take a long, long walk.

For the first quarter mile you are whipped. The realization that you are a complete failure reaches every little quivering corpuscle. Your gaze is humble when it falls upon junk dealers and garbage men. This is the crucial moment. If you can pull yourself over this hump, you are a writer. Going over the hump means that you leave behind you any idea that your written word is sacred. It means too that you can view the novel critically, sanely, with detachment. It is no longer a lyrical masterpiece. Neither, you have begun to realize, is it a hopeless hulk which brands you forever as the little gent who thought he could write. You have cleared the hump. You have achieved the dogged conviction that the novel is fundamentally sound, based on a good creative idea. You have realized that what the novel needs is *rewriting*.

As soon as you have this fact firmly in mind, your brain begins to stir up scattered ideas. You think of ways to make Terry Williams something more of a man and less of a foop (Foop is not in Webster. A foop is the only word that fully describes Terry Williams). If you take that infernal collegiate pipe out of his lean tanned jaw, and make him something less than omniscient, he might turn into more than a Boy Scout.

You're doing fine! You have taken the first big step in rewriting, The next step is even bigger-systematic analysis. Discover what portions of your manuscript maintain the sound progression of plot, what situations hold the drama and suspense you have tried to build, what scenes deal effectively with clues and motivations, With these as your standards, go after weaknesses which caused those "rereading blues."

If the third murder is superfluous, spare that gore! If the

cigarette clue is mouldy, get rid of it. If the closing chapter is dull, save the good ideas in it and junk the writing.

It is time to bring up replacements. But–how do I know exactly what's wrong and how do I fix it?

Well, here's the way it's done. First of all I'm going to show you some serious weaknesses to watch out for. Then I'm going to tell you how, after you've cut out these weaknesses, you can fill the gaps. As an example, I'm going to use the rewriting I did on my novel, *The Black Seven*.

We can divide weaknesses into three kinds: faults of plot, faults of motivation, faults of character. Sometimes they can't be separated. But for the sake of convenience and clarity, I'm separating them.

Faults of plot. Vaguely, you are aware that there are weaknesses. Now let's get rid of that "vaguely." You must find out exactly what's wrong.

Here are two rule-of-thumb tests to apply to your plot.

1. Are there any *loose threads?* A loose thread is any scene, incident, plot sequence which does not contribute to the direct, forward movement of the plot. Sometimes it's a "wonderful idea" which you could not resist but which has no real bearing on the plot, is no more than a distracting digression. Test: *if the plot can get along without it–then its a loose thread.*

Or it may be a situation which *is* an integral part of the plot, but which is illogical–in the light of plain common sense it looks "fishy." For example, your heroine, sees a man prowling in the garden at night. Next morning she "just doesn't happen" to mention this fact to her family. Consequently, Uncle Dudley and the police are puzzled for two days by the disappearance of the old sundial. But the reader isn't puzzled; he's exasperated by this "fishy" situation, this loose thread.

Ruthlessly cut out all loose threads. If a situation does not push the plot forward and push it forward convincingly, it will have to go.

2. Do your beginning and your ending function properly; i.e., begin and end? Remember, the beginning of your novel must hook the reader's interest, must arouse his curiosity by suggesting what is to come — murder, violence, mayhem. Your ending must

---

completely satisfy that curiosity.

Take your beginning. Does your opening chapter hold the promise of conflict or menace or violent death or fear? In other words, does it arouse the reader's interest by showing him that your fundamental plot situation is loaded with dynamite and that sometime there's going to be an explosion? You need not begin with a dead body, but your first chapter should have some promise of *impending trouble in it.*

Early in the novel your reader must know everything about the past of your characters which is necessary to explain the events you are dealing with. Two dangers here: Have you spent too much time on this antecedent material and bogged down the novel? Have you neglected this background and confused the reader? You must strike a balance. If your opening does not both look to the future and explain the past-rewrite.

As for the ending: have you explained everything? That's the crucial question. Let's expand it a little: have you explained everything and at the same time not bored the reader with a forty-page monologue in which the detective wallows in his own cleverness while the yokels gasp and rub their bare feet in the oriental rugs? You see, you must strike a balance again. Explain everything but don't write an explanatory essay. If your ending falls in either direction—rewrite.

Suppose you've spotted and cut out a loose thread of the "fishy" kind—a straw obstacle, let us say, like your heroine's failure to mention the mysterious prowler in the garden. This is the easiest kind to rewrite, because very often you will find you need nothing to take its place—jerking it out is enough. For example, Hyacinth, your heroine, immediately reports the prowler who swiped the old sundial with the mysterious numerals on its brass edge. Now your detective and the police can immediately start to hunt for him, to figure out why. You've speeded the pace; you've quickened the reader's interest.

Let's take two possibilities which have forced you to face the rewriting of your beginning.

a.   It lacks menace, that sense of impending trouble, that foreshadowing of mysterious death which the detective fan expects. Try to begin your novel *later*, i.e., nearer to the actual moment of death or violence. If the murder is committed on July twenty fifth, see if you can't begin the novel on July twenty-fourth-instead of April first. Here's a rough criterion. Begin your novel as close to the murder as you can-without having to bog it down with too much explanation of antecedent action. For example, don't start by showing Aunt Hester, the tight-fisted matriarch, serenely meddling with the lives of her family. Show her already stricken by a fear she cannot entirely conceal. For the past week she has found every night on her pillow a little drawing of an old woman done to death in a variety of ways, one night by hanging, another by the knife, etc. Begin the novel at a point where the shadow of violence is already unmistakably upon the opening situation and the reader's appetite is whetted by the promise of what is to come.

b.   Is your beginning confused because the reader does not know what has happened in the past? What to do? Make a list of all those things happening before the novel begins which the reader must know about. They will be quarrels and marriages and family relationships. They will be anything without the knowledge of which the reader cannot follow the action of the present.

Now, all the items on this list you must inject into the novel before it has got well under way. Not in a lump—you'll smother the reader's interest. These items must be laid in, a strand here, a strand there, naturally. There are three chief ways to accomplish this: (1) by having your characters talk about the past-clearly; (2) by having your characters or one character think about the past; and (3) by your own explanations—author's point of view which you attach to characters as you introduce them or which you embody in letters, memoirs, wills, newspaper accounts, etc. One of these devices or a combination of them should work.

As for the ending of your novel, which also needs rewriting—make another list. Check through the novel suspiciously. Put down- every clue, every motivation of character, every mysterious event which has not already been cleared up by the detective in the course of the novel. All these, then, must be accounted for in your ending. Note this, however. All trivial clues, all smaller mysteries should have been previously cleared up. And this explanation must be as simple as possible. Don't gloat over your detective's cleverness.

In order to present several specific examples of my own rewriting for plot flaws, I must give here a 200-word resumé of *The Black Seven*.

The Black Seven concerns a bright twelve-year-old boy, a talking starling, some mysterious objects called Black Babies, a thirteen-year-old sex job named Jeannine, houseful of rats, some pornographic literature, and a raft of disreputable Twiggs.

The boy, Roderick (Drawers to his friends) Random, becomes involved with the Twigg family because he has appropriated the tool shed on the old and disused Twigg property for his "Gas House." At the opening of the novel Casper Twigg (a great prankster) has at last discovered who murdered old Tobias Twigg five years before and moves back into Twigg Terrace as the first step in baiting the rest of the Twiggs.

But setting the Twiggs by their ears proves an unprofitable business. Casper is murdered—in the Gas House. Thenceforth Drawers visits, or is visited by, or tangles with the following Twiggs: Jasper, adopted, who pities himself and doesn't wash very often; Dulcet, whose psyche has been analyzed; Toby, who runs a candy factory and paints in the surrealistic school; Tammany, whose legs Drawers approves of; Cannas, who has a refrigerator full of cold beer; and Cannas' daughter Jeannine, the aforementioned sex job. There is also a detective who plays his part straight.

In rereading the novel for flaws I spotted one loose thread immediately. It concerned a plot sequence built around the existence of Dulcet Twigg's illegitimate daughter. Since Dulcet is murdered long before the daughter is even discovered and since the daughter plays no part in the novel except to show why Dulcet might have been suspected of murder, her appearance in the book leads to a blind alley. But before I tossed the scene into the discard I asked myself just what had been accomplished in those pages. Clearly, three things: (1) the detective was out of the way so that more hanky-panky could go on during his absence from town; (2) he pried some important information out of Tammany and furthered their love affair; (3) the scene provided suspense because the preceding chapter had ended with Drawers' lying unconscious in the rain behind Twigg Terrace.

Since I wished to maintain these three results, it was necessary to write a new scene which would accomplish the same things. It could be a relatively simple scene, but it couldn't be trivial. And since it was to take place at the same time that Drawers was lying unconscious in the weeds, the scene had to include the same weather conditions that prevailed for Drawers—a cloudburst.

It was the cloudburst that gave me the hint. The detective of my novel drives a decrepit old racing car with no top but with a propensity for flooding in a severe rain. Why not have him caught in the cloudburst! And why is he out driving in the country when he should be in town tightening up his case? Why, because he is chasing Tammany's car. And why is Tammany running away from him? Because she is annoyed that he is following her. Now wait a moment. This must be worked out carefully; there are troublesome details. Let's go back just a little way.

Suppose Tammany visits Jasper's apartment (I want to add another Tammany-Jasper quarrel scene, anyway) and comes away from there in considerable pique. And suppose she runs into the detective right outside Jasper's door—he has been trying to find her all day—but stalks past him in her indignation. Suppose he follows her. She has a temper: when she sees the racing car behind her, she decides to give it a good chase. She heads for the country, the detective after her. The cloudburst bursts. The detective's car stalls. Tammany picks up the water-logged detective. She is still furious. By the time he talks her into a gentler mood and pries out some information which he needs, gobs of time has passed and I can now go back and pick up Drawers where I left him unconscious in the weeds.

You see that I have accomplished my three points in this new scene: (1) the detective is out of the way; (2) he gets further information from Tammany and advances their love affair; and (3) the suspense is still present. And (4), I have got rid of a very loose end. You will note how I generated new ideas for the scene by association, a sort of "chain reaction." One idea, *if studied carefully,* will lead to another. With a little practice you can easily get your own "chain reaction" going.

Just one more example of a plot deficiency, this one having to do with the opening pages of the novel. In the original manuscript of *The Black Seven* there was a will, but its contents were revealed vaguely by characters as the novel progressed. Here was a background fact that all the Twiggs knew and that the reader deserved to know, yet a specific accounting of what was in the will was delayed until the middle of the novel. Furthermore, since the will carried mention of the mysterious Black Babies and made telling references to the Twigg family, it could well serve as a suspenseful beginning of the novel. So I gathered up the shards of information concerning the will, worded the document as old Tobias with his crabbed humor would have done, and presented it in the second chapter, thereby achieving that prime requisite of a detective novel—an early menace.

Let's come to motivation. The actions of your characters are not always clear or convincing, you realize. Sometimes they turn into puppets. They do things because the plot demands that they do them—and for no other reason. How can you spot and cut out this sort of fault? First you must realize that it is a fault in *motivation*. Remember, motivation is an accounting for actions in terms of believable human behavior, human desires, prejudices, fears. You have good motivation when you have satisfied the reader as to why people do things.

You must yourself turn detective. Go through your novel armed with the single question—WHY? Query all the significant actions of your characters. Why does Uncle Dudley insist upon talking about the signs of the Zodiac? Why does Aunt Hester go through the rain at eleven o'clock at night to visit the old woodshed? Why? Don't pretend that the lack of an answer won't matter—just this once. If your novel does not give a reason for the character's action—a reason which any intelligent reader will accept, knowing what he does of the character—then put that action down on your list. When you finish, you will have a list of actions which are not motivated or are improperly motivated. You will have a precise explanation for why the novel "seemed' weak or foggy in places. And now you must rewrite.

This should not be so difficult. These faulty motivations can, in general, be divided into two kinds: actions which have no motivation because they have no business in the novel-not even Shakespeare, with all his knowledge of the human heart, could account for them—and actions which are essential to the novel but for which you have failed to supply a proper motivation (because, since they are "necessary to the plot," you have probably presented them as if the mere necessity were an explanation!). When you spot the first kind, cut them out. The novel will be the stronger. If Uncle Dudley talks about signs of the Zodiac only because it occurred to you that the Zodiac had some beautifully mysterious connection with a sundial (soon to be pilfered), then cut that talk. In short, you will solve some of your motivation faults by excising altogether the unnecessary actions which exposed them.

F inally, we come to characterizations. In the modern detective novel the emphasis is more on character.

Take each of your major characters in turn. Put their names on separate sheets of paper. Now go through the novel and write down, under each character, everything that he does, says, thinks about, and everything which you, as author, say about him. You will then have a complete sketch of what the reader knows about each character.

Study this sketch carefully and ask yourself three questions:

1. Is the past life of this character clear—i.e., do we have that information about his earlier life (before the novel begins) which is necessary to explain his present conduct? Is his relationship to the other characters clear from the beginning? If he is one of two sons, for example, is it clear that he is the adopted one? If not, that information must be worked in as near the beginning as possible (see above on the opening of the novel).

2. Is the character an individual, not a creature of straw? Sometimes a difficult question to decide. Ask yourself this-is the character only a dummy identified by a "tag"? Beginning writers tend to "establish" characters by the fact that they continually smooth their oiled hair or wiggle their ears when they get excited or use stock phrases as, "Gosh all golly!" A good tag is helpful but it is not enough. Reveal the special quality of your character *by what he says and by what he does and by what he thinks.* To do this you may have to expand scenes or write new ones but it must be done.

Remember, if a character is an authentic and living individual in your mind, his authenticity and vitality must be translated to your book in conversation and thought and action. If he is not alive even in your mind, if you discover from studying your character sketch that he is an automaton, then rebuild him. Think of people you know. It is from your knowledge of people that character building comes. You are not going to rebuild your character into a replica of your Cousin Harry (Cousin Harry won't like it when he reads the book and besides there are traits in Cousin Harry which won't fit), but you will, perhaps, give him Cousin Harry's fundamental temperament and personality—or Cousin Harry's hatred of overstuffed furniture:

In "*The Black Seven*" for instance, Toby Twigg, consisted, in the rough draft, chiefly of a long, pale upper lip which was squeezed, pulled, rubbed, and smoothed in turn. How could I turn that lip into a real person? First of all, by *thinking* of Toby as a real person who was doing real things: I had indicated that he was a painter—but only indicated it. So I asked myself what sort of a picture Toby would paint. I described that picture. Then I gave him a little fame in the form of a letter from an art gallery and let him react to it. The first thing I knew, I had a real person instead of a long, pale upper lip traveling through the novel.

3. *Do the characters stay "in character"?* Does Aunt Hester always act like the sort of person you've convinced the reader Aunt Hester is? Study your sketch. Any conversations, actions, thoughts which are not "in character" will stand out in contrast with the true development of Aunt Hester's character as you have jotted it down. Remove all such psychological incongruities. Occasionally you will need no substitute—the episode is better omitted altogether. Perhaps, however, the psychologically correct action or reaction is necessary. In that case, restudy your sketch of Aunt Hester, then put her in the situation and see what she, instead of the impostor who had usurped her place, would really do or say. Then rewrite it in your novel.

In other words, by making this sketch of each character and then applying the three questions, you have accomplished the two important steps in rewriting: you have created a standard, a measuring rod, by which to discover the bad elements of characterization which must be cut out. You have also provided yourself with material which will help to show you what you should put in its place.

I followed this method in rewriting *The Black Seven*. For example, by studying these character sketches I discovered that my characters were not clearly introduced to the reader.

A solid month of such rewriting activity as I have indicated above made me realize that I had penetrated at least one secret of the devious and diabolical writing craft: the difference between authoring an unsold manuscript and a published novel is frequently not a matter of "inspiration" or "talent" or "luck" or "divine afflatus." It sometimes consists simply (*who* said "simply") in having the stamina—and the method—to follow-through, to build a fundamentally sound structure into a good novel.

When I finished rewriting "*The Black Seven*," my husband wrung me out and hung me over the clothesline to dry in the wind. From a novel of 285 pages I had cut completely 60 pages and added 85 new ones. In 300 pages, then, there were exactly 25 that were virginal, except for the fact that the page numbers were changed.

See what I mean by rewriting?

To recap the highlights:

1. Put it aside for a while. Then read it through.
2. Look out for "loose threads;" events that don't move the plot forward, or ones that don't make sense.
3. Review the beginning and end. Does the beginning hook? Does the ending satisfy?
4. Check the motivations of every major character for major events.

TRY WISHFUL THINKING!

A Formula for fiction

By Kitte Turmell

This article comes from the November, 1938 issue of Writer's Markets & Methods.

*(A*n interview with Dr. Lloyd C. Douglas, author of "Magnificent Obsession," "Forgive Us Our Trespasses," "Green Light," and "White Banners." His latest novel, "Disputed Passage," is now appearing as a continued story in Cosmopolitan Magazine.)

"Wishful thinking is the best basis for good plots! The stories that grip your interest are those that picture all the experiences you've never had the courage to try, all the far-flung places you've never dared explore, all the fascinating people you've always hoped to meet! Just put your own unfulfilled wishes into words and you'll have absorbing material for successful fiction!"

That's the advice of Dr. Lloyd Douglas, the only American author who ever achieved the unique distinction of having three of his books on a national list of best-sellers at the same time!

At the beautiful Bel Air home that best-seller books built, Dr. Douglas told me why wishful thinking is an aid to any writer.

"Too many beginners try to transfer real facts into fiction and then wonder why their plots seem stilted and colorless! One must use facts, of course, but good stories aren't written about you or anyone you know without considerable changing. Unless your plot theme appeals to your own imagination, it is not likely to absorb the interest of the reader!"

"I don't think an author should worry unduly about a plot anyway. After all, he's entitled to as much suspense as the reader. Of course sometimes there is too much suspense if the first installments are in print before the author decides how it will turn out. That's as dangerous as doing a crossword puzzle in invisible ink! When I start a story I never have any idea how it will develop. I just let the plot spin along from chapter to chapter and take care of itself."

"But Doctor Douglas!" I exclaimed. "Aren't there many prominent writers who never think of beginning to write a story until they have the plot worked out in detail in their mind and—"

"Right," he cut in. "I'm simply telling you how I work. Every writer must experiment and find the method that suits him best. Writing habits are a matter of conditioning anyway and it is unwise to try to change them. For instance, a man who must scribble his ideas on scraps of paper while he's performing other work, becomes accustomed to doing his first drafts in longhand. A man who has leisure to do his first writing during spare time is likely to use a typewriter. I do all my first drafts on this noiseless typewriter because I like to see how the words look on the page, in order to correctly gauge the length of sentences and paragraphs. Eye-appeal, for the reader, is more important than most writers realize, you know."

Dr. Douglas has also discovered that he must follow a regular schedule, in order to ward off the temptations for distraction that beset most writers. He is at his desk at 8 every morning and works until 3, without even taking time out for lunch because it makes him sleepy. Sometimes in a whole day he writes only 200 words he considers worth keeping; he discards 10,000 words for every 1,000 that he retains.

"I may revise each chapter many times but once it is completed I never go back to it. I find that most chapters fall naturally into three episodes so I handle each episode as a separate unit and repolish it before I try to fit the entire chapter together with connecting sequences."

"Do you have your readers in mind as you write?" I asked, thinking of the millions who know Dr. Douglas' novels by heart and have made their kindly philosophy a design for living.

"I have three or four men in mind, always," he confided. "If I'm handling controversial material, I consider the probable reactions of a certain brilliant Ann Arbor professor. If it's a love scene I try to imagine whether it would seem effective or a little too sentimental to a sparkling, half-cynical publisher who is another unseen mentor.

"I like music while I work; so I have music from a panotrope in the drawing room piped in here. When I press a button the records play for three hours without stopping." He beamed pridefully, as he sauntered across the soft red Oriental rug in his sunny study, paneled with knotty pine, and started a red-seal symphony record. The easy grace of the classical music matched the rhythm of the smooth-flowing prose that distinguishes all the Dr. Douglas books.

"How can an inexperienced writer perfect his style?" I asked.

"For one thing, by remembering that the modern vogue to transform adjectives into adverbs can be shockingly badly done." He grinned like a schoolboy. "My last sentence, you'll notice, is a good example of what I mean. Remember that most adjectives have been abused like beasts of burden until they're wobbly in the knees from carrying too much weight. Extravaganzas like 'super colossal' have become meaningless."... This from the author who made the adjective "magnificent" go around the world as half-title for his first book, "Magnificent Obsession," now in its 48th printing!

"Revise for brevity, clarity, euphony, and strength, if you wish to achieve artistic style, but don't polish a phrase so bare that it means nothing to anyone except yourself," he continued earnestly. "Don't rewrite so often that you rub off the skin, the glow, the stardust.

"Don't be verbose. Most of the manuscripts sent to me for criticism could be strengthened by taking 45 words away from every 50. Often I come across a 7,000 word story that I know doesn't deserve over 1,500 words."

Dr. Douglas believes that every writer must master the fundamentals of style, before attempting any variations.

"Only a recognized social leader can afford to put her elbows on a table and munch a chop-bone in public. Even a Hemingway cannot risk a radical departure in style unless the reader feels that the writer knows thoroughly all the conventions that he flaunts.

"Only too often, a writer does his first book because he has something to tell... and all the others because he has something to sell!

"Once a writer is established, there is nothing he could

conceive of so preposterous that it will not find a market," he mused. "That is why an author who has achieved some success must be more meticulous than ever, in his stories. It is my belief that every author has just one important story to tell anyway. He may present it through different characters, in a variety of settings, with contrasting dialogue, but it's still the same basic story and when the public wearies of that story the author should stop writing. That applies to me, too," he added humbly.

My eyes wandered to an open book-shelf bright with fresh copies of "Magnificent Obsession," "Forgive Us Our Trespasses," "Green Light," and "White Banners," printed not only in English but in various foreign languages. On a table nearby was a copy of the first magazine installment of Dr. Douglas' latest novel, "Disputed Passage." On the desk, a marked copy of a glowing review of a motion picture version of one of Dr. Douglas' beloved books. He fingered the newspaper thoughtfully.

"People keep asking me why I don't write scenarios instead of novels, because some of my stories have been adapted to the screen. But I tell them I have no reason to think I have any talent for scenarios... or I would have tried them long ago. I don't believe a writer should depart from his own particular field anyway. Find the form of writing to which you are most suited and stay with it. That's the truest wisdom that can be acquired in any craft!"

It was by chance that Dr. Douglas discovered the talent for full-length fiction that has placed him in the top rank of American novelists. He was writing a religious essay on the spiritual values derived from helping others, when he decided that the thoughtful paragraphs were getting too ponderous. He started trying to enliven the essay with dialogue and that's how "Magnificent Obsession" was born.

"After that book achieved such surprising success... and the small publishing house that first issued it surrendered the plates to a large publishing house in the East in order to handle the mounting demand... I dusted off a short story that had been rejected, long before that, without even letters of comment from the editors. I retyped the first page of the story, soiled by migrations, and sold it to a magazine that had formerly refused it... for $1,000!

So don't be discouraged by those first refusals. After all you wouldn't expect to win an architectural contest on your first drawing... or to play a sonata after just six piano lessons. Writing is brimful of headache and heartache, and only the self-confident survive."

"Do you ever want to get away from it all?"

"I wouldn't say that... I love to write, but I'll admit that I'm anticipating our cruise to South America. We're leaving tomorrow morning, you know; my wife is packing right now. We'll be away until late January."

As the hospitable Dr. Douglas bade me goodbye there was a discerning twinkle in his eye and I suspect he guessed that right then I was doing some wishful thinking of my own... wishing I too, were on my way to Rio de Janeiro. I also suspect he knew that I'd start mulling over his advice... follow his formula for success... and imagine as a theme for my next story what might happen if I were leaving on that coveted cruise.

Because... don't be forgetting the Dr. Douglas dictum.

"Wishful thinking is the best basis for interesting plots."

This one is short and sweet, but still has a few good ideas.
- "Unless your plot theme appeals to your own imagination, it is not likely to absorb the interest of the reader!" If you're bored writing it, then it's going to feel boring to the reader.
- Dr. Douglass was a pasntser, writing without an outline.
- He also suggests finding a method of writing that works for you, then sticking to that.
- His own routine involved writing at the same time every day.

How to Write Love Scenes

By Minna Bardon

Originally appeared in May 1933 Writer's Digest.

Impulsively, your sweetheart sweeps you into his arms. His lips press yours, drinking in their sweetness, thrilling you through and through.

"Dear little girl!" he whispers huskily, his lips upon your hair. "How I love you, darling!"

Happily, you let yourself relax in his strong arms. Troubles are gone. The future is filled with rich promise of untold joy. You raise your lips, sweet, soft, tremulous, to him as his arms tighten around you and draw you close. He kisses you for a magical moment that fills the world with ecstatic romance.

You no like? Then you don't belong in one of my pulp stories (or in one of your own).

Because that's the way to make love in pulp paper love fiction. Above is a typical pulp paper scene.

There must be glamor in these tales — and plenty of it. Ecstatic emotion, too (or you'll get your story back with a few dismal words about "unreality" and vagueness).

At a time like this you can't afford to take a chance with your yarns, unless you write for the joy of the writing and get your satisfaction from filing your manuscripts in a dud drawer instead of kissing them goodbye and endorsing your publisher's checks.

Pick up one of the standard love pulps, open it to almost and page and let's see what happens:

> ... *How good it seemed to feel his arms around her, to know that he loved her.*

After kissing her for a long, delicious moment, Garry drew back and looked at her. "Darling, do you know that soon you'll be my wife? That you'll be mine ans never again will we need to be parted?"

Their lips clung together again in a kiss that seemed to touch with delicate fingers Mary's very soul and assure her of a life of love and happiness. And suddenly she knew, that with Garry as her companion life held no fears or temptations for her. She was content and Garry, kissing her again, and feeling the yielding warmth of her lips, thanked heaven for the fact that Mary was his to love and adore for all time.

Y ou don't like to write stuff like this? You think it's terrible? You wouldn't sign your name to such an effusion? Then take all of your aspirations toward writing pulp paper love fiction, wrap them in a tidy package, and give them to poor Aunt Lil for Christmas.

Writing needs restraint? Writing shouldn't be sloppily full of sentimentality? Would you rather treat your love scenes in somewhat the same fashion as Jane Austen did hers?

Let's take this same scene and see how *not* to write it.

"... Mary loved Garry and she wanted him to kiss her. He put his arms around her and told her that he loved her. After kissing her, he asked her to marry him and she said that she would. They kissed again and she knew that she would be happy married to Garry, and Garry knew that he would be happy married to her."

I 've seen stories (and they were supposed to be love stories) written with just about as much ecstatic emotion as this last scene.

Not very long ago I said to one aspiring young writer who had handed me a page not unlike the one I have just quoted: "Don't you believe in love? Or is it your heroine who hasn't a love emotion to her name?"

The writer blushed and laughed. "I can't write stuff like you see in those magazines. They act like such silly nuts. Who cares whether my heroine's heart palpitates when she looks at the hero's curly hair and what difference does it make whether the hero kisses the heroine tremulously or ecstatically?"

It *does* make a difference. You are writing your pulp paper love story for a girl *who wants to know everything* about a love scene. She wants to know where it took place. If your people are walking in the moonlight, say so. If they are standing on the deck of a yacht, say that. If they are behind the counter of a five and ten cent store, don't forget to mention that. If he says, "I love you," three times, don't think that your reader will find the words monotonous.

She dreams about a lover of her own (an imaginary lover) who will come wooing with the words "I love you" on his lips six times every day and seven on Sunday. Let's take another example. A little unusual. Let's see...

Love in a snow-storm? How's that?

"...We'll walk away together and be married. Tell me—will you be glad?"

Glad? She didn't have to speak. The answer was in her shining eyes.

It was snowing hard now. Soft, cottony flakes that fell on her pink, flushed cheeks, and clung to her sweet mouth.

"Little snow fairy," Jim laughed, and kissed them clear.

Breathlessly their lips clung. Then they turned and made their way towards the lighted town. The snow clouds walked with them; took form; changed into the phantoms of the coming years. Little years, big years, happy years; sad years; marching beside them. But Lynn and Jim unconscious of their wistful escort, and uncaring, walked on together.

Life was before them, and love...

T hat's the way you'd write your scene if you wanted your story to sell. You wouldn't handle it in a more matter of fact fashion without the emotional glamor. You wouldn't say anything like this:

> *...It was snowing outside and they met and walked on together, enjoying themselves. Jim wanted to know if Lynn would take a walk with him then and get married. He asked if she would be glad when they were married.*

> *She didn't answer him because she knew he knew that she wanted to marry him anyhow.*

> *The snow was still falling very beautifully as they walked along and then he stopped and kissed her and they walked on together after that.*

P retty bad, isn't it? Even worse than the almost lyrically hysterical passages that you and I have often laughed at in the love scenes of some pulp paper magazines.

I've read one love story (inspired, probably, by "*The Sheik*") in which the lovers talked like two comradely schoolboys setting out for a stroll across the town. I've read another with practically the same setting, in which the lovers did everything but swoon from their ecstatic emotion right there on the desert sands. Of the two, the latter sounded much more authentic. After all, you could feel that the lovers were lovers and not just two names written on manuscript paper with the aid of a portable typewriter and ten agile fingers.

Here's another love scene that may help:

> *... Through the dim mellowness of the old house a woman's voice, high and clear and sweet, floated suddenly, lifted in an old sweet song of love and springtime :*

> *"Once in Maytime-once in dewy Maytime—Two lovers met. Their eyes—their lips..."*

> *"Like us," Jane whispered against his shoulder. "Like us in*

the dawn that morning."

Fred drew her closer. "Like this, Jane," he replied against her lips. "Like this!"

She could feel the beat of his heart beneath her cheek. She thrilled to the muted note of admiration in his voice...

Isn't that a perfect love scene for the day dream of a young girl? It isn't only the telephone operators and the girls behind the notion counters who want love to happen to them. All girls do and you are writing for the simplest desires of the average girl.

Wouldn't it be foolish to avoid the emotional and the glamor? It would be a mistake to say matter-of-factly:

...Somebody was singing a song in the house. It was a woman and they heard her. The song was something that reminded them of themselves and the first time they met, and they said something about it. When Jane reminded Fred of the time that the two of them met he put his arms around her and kissed her...

It wouldn't be a bit more subtle but it would certainly be lots more salable if you'd put a little emotion into their speeches. For instance, take a look at this:

...He put his arm around her, drawing her against his shoulder. He lifted her chin with his free hand. A deep shiver of ecstasy ran through the girl at the sight of that dark, earnest face, those glowing eyes, so near.

"I love you," Andrew said. "And I believe that I can make you love me. Give me a chance, my darling! Let me come here every day and tell you how much I love you-how I tried to hate you and could not"... She pressed a kiss upon his mouth... "I love you to death already!"

The same elements of glamor and emotion are in this paragraph. Now let's talk about these scenes and see what they have in common. Let's make a formula for them if we can.

There is, in each love scene, a definite statement of love. "I love you," is said at least once. (And the man who says "I love you" always has honorable intentions in these standard love pulps.)

Each of the scenes is written from the point of view of the girl. She is always happy in the man's love. She is always tremulous during the process of the love scene. Sometimes she is surprised at his love-avowal but always she is blissfully happy.

He always puts his arms around her (you must not take this for granted either) and draws her close to him. There is always, somewhere in the love scene, the intimation of the permanency of the love. (We girls do like to be certain that love lasts forever).

He says (if this is near the end of a story): "Will you marry me?" And he always insists on having the wedding soon. Tomorrow is a splendid time for any pulp paper wedding. Today is still better. Next week is a long time away and longer than six months is just an impossibility.

The hero is always sincere and strong and earnest. He often shows traces of past jealousy (although he knows now that there was nothing really to be jealous about).

The girl is usually shivering with ecstasy or trembling with delight or crying with happiness.

She thrills to the man, to the moonlight (if any) or the storm (if any) or the sunlight (there often is sunlight).

You mustn't, if you're writing scenes like this, say simply, "He kissed her."

You must say:

"She raised her lips, soft, tremulous, to his," or "He felt the yielding warmth of her lips." Or "Breathlessly their lips clung." Or "His lips were against hers in an ecstasy, new and age-old."

You see how to handle these scenes? Never be matter-of-fact. Always mention the emotion that the girl feels, rather than merely the thing she does or says. Don't ever omit the exact statements, "I love you," and "Will you marry me?" Keep your reader feeling that the tinkle of wedding bells and the fragrance of orange blossoms are just around the corner. Mention your setting only as a background to your love scene. Make it evident that your heroine is beautiful and charming (just as if no girl was ever loved except when she had just invested in a new dress and a permanent wave). Be certain that your hero is handsome or worthy (usually both), and that he is madly in love with the heroine (in a perfectly nice way, of course.)

So far we have mentioned only the absolutely serious love scenes. They are the kind you meet most often in love pulps. But there is another acceptable variety. You couldn't exactly call it humorous, and yet there is a certain light touch about it. You feel that the hero and heroine are seriously in love (for a lifetime, naturally), but they are a little playful about it. Sometimes the hero is tenderly amused and indulgent in a sort of David Copperfield-Dora sort of way.

Here are a few samples of this type: (I'll take them from some published stories of my own that happen to be on my desk.)

In one story the boy and girl have just met again after a long absence :

> ... *"When you sit there looking at me like that, Joan, I can believe that anything is possible. I can imagine that miracles will come from around the next corner and stride up to me on the street saying, 'Come along, Tony. We're happening to you, we miracles.' Do you think that I'm falling in love with you again?"*

That's just the tenderly playful touch that you can add. But don't forget the kisses and the emotions and the tremulous touches, too. They all belong. And don't be too playful. Love is a serious problem in these stories. Keep your humor for *Ballyhoo;* except for these mild, tenderly, amused passages. Like this, for instance :

> *"In other words, I can't love anybody but you. And if you dare remind me, one single time up to our fiftieth anniversary, how foolish I was in believing that I ever loved anybody but you, I'll ...*

> *"What will you do?" he asked, with the glow of a new happiness on his tired face.*

> *"I'll kiss you," she answered, and suited the action to the word.*

T his is the only moderately humorous passage. The rest has the same quantities of tremulous words and tender kisses and detailed love making as the other samples I've given. Here's still another one that's "tenderly amused":

> *"You foolish darling, what's the matter? Have you been burning down orphan asylums or stealing pennies from blind men's cups? Whichever it is, I'll still love you and want to marry you."*

I can't impress too strongly upon your minds that you mustn't change your formula when you add the "tenderly amused" paragraphs occasionally. (Don't do it *more* than occasionally.) Just add them to the rest of the mixture, like nuts to chocolate fudge. After all, the formula is complete without the "tenderly amused" bits.

And just to give yourself a sample that has almost every ingredient that you need in a love scene formula, copy this one down in your notebook. (It isn't my own, by the way.):

> *"... Hope?" she breathed fearfully. "Yes, the hope that you will make me the happiest man in the world. Isobel" — he drew her into his arms – "Oh, my very dear, I have loved you for months and I didn't know it . . . Will you be my wife?"*

> *"Oh, I can't believe it! I can't believe it's true," she cried, a sob in her voice...*

> *Tenderly he drew her closer and, bending, kissed her soft cheek, kissed each eye closed, and finally kissed the lovely redness of her lips. As Isobel relaxed in his embrace and surrendered herself to his caresses, she knew that as long as the man she loved believed she was innocent, the rest of the world did not matter. And, raising her lips again for his kiss, she knew that there was no need of further words or explanations they had their love and that was enough."*

D on't think, please, that I'm recommending these love scenes as samples of perfect writing. I have purposely chosen slightly exaggerated examples of the points I wanted to make. You may be able to get every one of these necessities into your love scene without making your paragraphs stilted and self-conscious. But you must not sacrifice emotion to restraint. It is better far to be a little bit too emotional than to be too restrained. Remember that these girls do not recognize restrained emotion.

If a girl seems calm and collected to them, they do not consider that she may simply have self-control enough to hide her emotions. If she has emotion she must show it —especially in her love scenes.

Remember your formula :

Let your sweetheart sweep you into his arms. Let his lips press yours, drinking in their sweetness, thrilling you through and through.

"Dear little girl," he'll murmur, or "Sweet little darling," or words to that effect. "Will you be my wife?"

Happily, you let yourself relax in his strong arms. All your troubles vanish. The future is filled with rich promise of untold joy. You raise your lips, soft and trembling, to him as his arms tighten around you and draw you close. He kisses you for a magical moment that fills the world with sunbright romance.

Follow that formula for yourself. Sit down and write variations of it if you want to get yourself into the mood for writing this type of material. Stage the same love scene on a mountain top or on a dance floor. Put your lovers in a rocket-ship bound for Mars or in a Rolls Royce bound for the opera. It's good practise—if you want to write pulp love fiction.

But don't forget the echo of wedding bells and the scent of the orange blossoms. Give all of your love scenes perfectly good intentions.

So this article is obviously quite dated. I don't read much romance, but I'm sure the genre as a whole must have moved on a little bit by now, right? The big lesson here is then: *Know the tropes for your genre.* Use them. Don't be afraid to.

Also, from a craft perspective, this could almost be an article about strengthening your verbs, with only romance examples.

How to Write True Detective Mysteries

By Douglas Lurton
Editor, Startling Detective Adventures

This article was originally published in the May, 1933 issue of Writers Digest.

W hen I undertake the writing of a true mystery story I usually have a rough formula in mind evolved from personally writing and editing many hundred true crime stories.

Circumstances frequently alter the method of procedure but the majority of cases published are written on the basis of a rough formula or outline such as the following:

1. Common methods of opening:

a.   The alarm or call for help, with its drama and action.

b.   Discovery of the crime when it is dramatic.

c.   Visualization of the commission of the crime with the drama and action involved.

d.   Officer being ordered to take up the baffling case.

e.   Setting of the scene. (Least desirable unless writer is experienced and skillful.)

f.   A combination of one or more of the above.

2 . The setting:

The scene is linked closely to the opening and is often interwoven with the beginning revelations. This requires a closeup of the scene of the crime starting with the body of the victim, the empty gem case, the kidnap spot, etc., and gradually taking in details of the room and the place and the locality, or starting with the locality and narrowing down to the center of interest.

3. Body of the story:

Deals with the dogged efforts of the detective to "crack" the mystery and the greater the obstacles are made to appear and the more baffling the case the better the story.

The preliminary search for clues, and to establish the identity of the victim (if not effectively established in the opening); first stories of witnesses or studying of theories; deduction from clues; consideration of possible motives.

Questioning of anyone who has anything to contribute to the solution, more detailed examination of old clues and new ones, study of weapons and possible finger prints.

Analysis of findings and deductions running throughout the body of the story and building toward the climax.

Backtracking for overlooked clues, if necessary, and the consideration and examination of various suspects and leads, always being careful to build up and hold suspense to avoid killing the climax.

Wherever it is logical, the discovery of the hot scent, followed doggedly by the detective whose viewpoint is held throughout.

4. The climax:

The drama and action of the arrest followed by confession or defiance that forces the detective to prove his case. The trial is frequently disposed of with a line or two if the case is clear, but is used dramatically if suspense has been held to place the climax in the trial.

To clarify the method of using such an outline we will analyze in detail a true mystery story recently published after being revised to overcome a common difficulty in such writing the difficulty being that as a matter of fact and rather early in the chronology the sheriff knows quite well who committed the crime in question.

Suspense is half of the reader value in true crime mysteries and it would be lost in the first hundred words or two if the writer did not adroitly maneuver the presentation, veil the real culprit and hold suspense to the last possible moment.

The true mystery story under analysis was "ghosted" for William S. Boone, former sheriff of Fulton county, Ohio, by Frank H. Ward who sensibly inserts bits of the sheriff's own homely detail that tend to convince the reader that the story is really being told by the officer. The big writer's problem in this story was to make suspense, for in the actual crime the sheriff knew the criminal from the start. This difficulty had to be overcome. Here's how:

The Lehman farm had been one of the show places of northwestern Ohio as far back as I could remember. There was nothing but blooded stock on the place, even including the chickens. The house and outbuildings were kept painted, the fences in repair. Beautiful trees sheltered the buildings.

This tranquil farm which was destined to be the scene of one of Ohio's most terrible tragedies lay on the Angola road, not far from the Michigan line. Thirty miles due east was the teaming city of Toledo, but it was far enough away not to disturb the peaceful content of Fulton county.

Young Fred Lehman had helped his father build up this splendid farm. That was when the youth was about twenty-six years old, and four years after his marriage to Grace Hall, one of the most beautiful girls in the state. A year or two later the elder Lehmans built a small house down Angola road a piece, on the edge of the acreage, and turned the farm over to Fred and his beautiful, young wife.

The young couple worked the farm together, the girl doing her full part to assist in the smooth management of the place. There was an air of contentment and well-being about the Lehman farm, a sense of peace that was to be utterly shattered by a murderous attack that shocked the nation.

It was between two and three A.M. on Monday, September 17, 1917, that Chet Mills, who lives on Angola road directly across from the Fred Lehman place, was aroused from his sleep by faint shouts. He listened intently for a few moments, then leaped from his bed. Mills jerked on his trousers and shoes and went out into the yard to investigate. He called to his wife and boys to light a lantern and follow.

The chill night wind stirred the branches of the ranks of trees which stood, sentinel-like, on the opposite side of the highway as Mills hurried toward the road. On the roadside, by his mailbox, Mills saw a dark object on the ground. He shouted, and from the figure came a faint answering call:

"Help me, Chet!" ...

(N)otice that in opening with the setting, the writer immediately promises "terrible tragedy" to snare interest. The setting is important as locations play an important part in the story later. This opening is an effective combination of methods "a" and "e". Time and place and characters have been well planted. The opening is calculated to grip reader curiosity as to what manner of crime is to shatter the peace of this country estate. As much drama, action, excitement as possible is crammed into the action detail that followed the call for help.)

Mills finds Fred Lehman bleeding, mumbling incoherently about "poor Grace." Mr. and Mrs. Mills carry the man to his own home and try to telephone for help.

No response. Mrs. Mills discovers beautiful Grace Lehman unconscious in bed and races to her own home to reach a usable telephone.

It was 5:15 A.M. when Deputy McQuillen and I arrived at the Lehman home. The first gleam of dawn was forcing a finger of light through the clouds. There were at least a dozen people there, but a cold silence seemed to grip the entire house.

I went at once into the bedroom. Grace Lehman was dead. There was a bullet in her right temple, and two tiny drops of blood on her pillow. She had died about twenty minutes after Mrs. Mills had found her, without regaining consciousness... (detail and descriptions of scene).

Three doctors were hovering tenderly around Fred Lehman. There was the family physician, another doctor he had called in, and Dr. Park S. Bishop, our coroner.

They told me that Lehman had been attacked and robbed by three thugs. I didn't wait to question Fred. I rushed to the Mills home and sent the alarm throughout our county...

Coming back across the road I noticed that the telephone wires had been cut just as they entered the Lehman house.

Fred Lehman was sitting up now in a chair. He had been shot in the left leg and left shoulder. There was a bruise on his left forehead, and three or four knife wounds on his breast.

Gradually I got the story from Fred. He and his wife had been to a family reunion at Swanton that Sunday. They had come home about dusk to do the chores. They had retired at about eight o'clock.

Fred, who had eaten too heartily at the reunion, was uncomfortable during the night, and got up several times. On the last occasion, while in the back yard, he heard a noise in the barn...

Investigating, Fred was overpowered by three thugs. He relates a detailed and exciting story of his struggles with the men who mentioned that they had been drafted for the army and weren't leaving for camp without money. They threatened to hang him and he struggled anew, receiving a blow on his head and the knife wounds before he broke free and in desperation ran to reach and defend his wife. Then he was shot down and left for dead. Knowing that wounded, he was no match for the gang, he crawled toward his neighbor's house for help and remembered nothing more until he regained consciousness in his own home. On the advice of physicians that he couldn't withstand the shock, knowledge of his wife's death was withheld.

(Here our investigator notes various details and questions the principal witness. And it is here that we first violate Van Dyne's ruling by withholding the fact that the knife wounds were on Fred's *left* chest and *his shirt was not slashed by the knife*. A definite clue is given to readers in mentioning that his other wounds were on the

left side but we avoid deductions that a right handed man inflicting wounds on himself would logically wound the left side and an assailant would have cut the shirt as well as the chest. As the story is written there is sympathy for the wounded husband. Theorizing on the location of the wounds at this point would destroy suspense. Instead, Fred is carefully veiled.)

As I puzzled over the attack and the possible motives, Fred's mention that his assailants had said they had been drafted and wouldn't leave him behind, came to my mind. I recalled that the second contingent of drafted men from our county was due to leave for Camp Sherman that week and that it had been rumored that Fred was not very enthusiastic about the prospect of being drafted and merged with a mass of conscripted men.

It seemed possible that some men of the county, irritated by Fred's comfortable situation and resenting his attitude toward the draft had decided to beat him. The theory held so far but could scarcely be expected to account for the murder of his charming young wife. Still puzzling over this I continued my investigation.

By now the Lehman home was packed with curious folk from miles around ... Among them were Leo Fenton and his wife, Alcy. Leo and Fred had been boyhood chums and schoolmates, and Grace and Alcy had known each other all their lives. The Fentons had moved to a farm a mile away about three years earlier and had supplemented their farm income by working out by the day. Leo as a hand, and Alcy at cleaning and cooking. Occasionally they had worked for their close friends, the Lehmans.

The Fentons had come over as soon as they heard about the tragic death of Grace and the beating of her husband ... But neither the Fentons nor other visitors offered anything of service to the investigation.

In a tour of inspection I found that an attempt had been

made to pry a screen from the bedroom window. I found Fred's empty pocketbook on the hayrack in the barn, and also the rope with the noose in it

I talked with the doctors ...

There is considerable discussion and conflicting theories of physicians as to whether death shot was fired while Grace Lehman lay in bed. The .22 bullet is found in her head. Fred is kept in ignorance of wife's death to avoid shock for day or two and weeps when finally informed of tragedy. Search is quickened. Murder weapon missing. A neighbor had seen a car with three men in it at 2:30 A.M., speeding without lights. Five men surrounded by posse in swamp, are found to be hunters. Warnings broadcast to beware of the marauders. It is learned that neither the Lehman dog nor the Mills dog had barked. This fact caused questioning of all former hired hands, one of whom was seriously suspected before he established a clear alibi. Thus clue after clue fell flat and as the investigation progressed plans were made for the funeral of Grace Lehman...

(Note that story is moved forward by detail, consideration of motives, findings of doctors, search for clues, false leads that were expanded somewhat to hold the suspense and spice the hunt. Here, too, important characters are "planted" for future use and the writer withholds the fact that Aley Fenton and Fred Lehman had been seen together, intimately, the suspense being held deliberately.)

There must have been fully eight hundred persons at the Lehman home... for the funeral interest centered in young widower, weak and pale from the wounds he had suffered... face grief stricken at the grave...

The suspense and tenseness of the moment reached a high pitch when the grave diggers began to fill in the grave with earth. It was at this moment that Deputy McQuillen and I quietly forced our wily through the crowd and approached the Lehman automobile. The crowd was hushed, so quiet one could hear the soft thud of a spadeful of dirt on Grace Lehman's casket, and the words came with startling clearness.

"We're going to take you to Wausean, Fred!"

The young widower, stunned by our statement, made no answer. We helped him out of his car, and he limped over to ours. If we had hoped that under the strain of viewing his beautiful wife for the last time he might talk, we were disappointed. Fred was silent. Not so the crowd. Several women screamed. A flurry, and the word spread that Fred Lehman had been arrested in connection with the murder of his wife. Arrested at her very grave. The murmur of surprise and excitement gradually changed to a murmur of indignation.

It was apparent that most of Fulton county was firmly behind Fred. His friends would not believe that he could have slain the beautiful girl he had led to the altar only a few years before. There was no motive for the act!...

Fred had a fine reputation... he and his wife had acted like sweethearts... there is a demonstration of protest against the arrest... true, the public didn't know all that the investigation had developed... but there was no clear-cut motive and that was a fact.

It was our theory that Lehman had killed his wife between 7:00 and 10:00 P.M. Sunday, the Mills family being away during that period. That would have accounted for their failure to hear shots during the period Fred set for the attack And we weren't forgetting that the Lehman and Mills dogs had been silent during the supposed attack.

During our investigation we had called on Morlon S. Griffin, county Surveyor, to make a plat of the crime scene. This plat showed that it was 281 feet from the barn where Fred said he was shot to the Mills' mailbox. That was a long pull for a wounded man.

The measurements also showed it was not more than 400

feet from the barn door to the Mills' bedrooms where four persons had slept undisturbed until Mr. Mills heard Lehman's faint shouts. But test shots could be heard half a mile away...

There is deduction from other clues. It is revealed that Fred's shirt was not cut when his breast was stabbed. The pistol is found under the milk house. There is conjecture as to how it got there, as an earlier search had not revealed it. Fred denies he ever had a revolver and confidently faced trial. No motive had yet been established. The trial opens and proceeds without event until a surprise witness is called...

(Note that suspense is held until the dramatic arrest at the grave. Even then the case is not cleared up for it seems to many Fred had been falsely accused. But now the investigator reveals various clues and deductions having an important bearing on the case but still the public believes Fred innocent and a motive is lacking so suspense still holds.)

This surprise witness was a comely young woman, well but plainly dressed... Young Lehman leaned forward and looked straight at her face for she was none other than Alcy Fenton, girlhood playmate of Grace Hall Lehman.

The crowded courtroom was hushed as she began her testimony. The testimony was not particularly exciting until it reached the point of detailed questioning regarding one of the pleasure trips taken by the Lehmans and the Fentons... The prosecutor asked her who had been in her company most of the time on that trip,

"Fred Lehman," she replied.

"While Fred and you were alone, what were you talking about?"

"Well, Fred told me stories," she answered.

"What were they?"

"I can't remember, but they were not Sunday school stories"...

A lcy Fenton reveals intimacy and kisses with Fred Lehman, snatched moments of love...

There was the motive, Fred Lehman had fallen in love with another woman, had carried on a serious flirtation with her... He had slain his wife, shot and slashed himself and invented the story of the raiders...

Lehman took the verdict and sentence without flinching-life imprisonment in the Ohio penitentiary at Columbus. He is there as this is written, serving as a trusty.

(The climax is reached when Alcy Fenton makes her startling revelations on the witness stand, a climax that would have been killed by earlier revelation of her intimacy with Lehman.)

A word of caution seems required in connection with manipulation of true stories to make them fit some of the requirements of fiction. Although *chronology* has been altered somewhat in the story analyzed it should be seen clearly that *facts* have not been changed. In case of a major manipulation of chronology it is well to take the editor into your confidence, explaining the changes made. Never alter the fundamental facts of a true crime story—there are too many readers eager to inform editors of such alterations.

Almost as important as the satisfactory writing of a given case is the selection of the case to be written. Avoid cases in which there is little drama or action or thrills; unimportant cases. Utilize cases in which the detective can be made to achieve something, instead of simply blundering along and finally receiving a telephone "tip off" from some unrelated source that solves the mystery but cancels all of his detecting and deducting. It is always advisable to query the editor before doing the detailed work on your story:

~

The rough outline for true mystery stories discussed in this article can be used to good advantage in plotting fiction stories as well. It should be pointed out that while the basic true mystery story is considered here the magazines in the field also publish expose articles, criminal career stories, occasionally outright true action stories and man-hunts that are not, strictly speaking, mystery stories.

The "Big Four" markets in the true mystery field are generally active, using old cases as well as some of the most recent "thrillers" in crime. The solved mystery predominates but occasionally unsolved crimes are published. Editors and circulation men have found that many readers of this type of magazine are women and generally the true case involving women finds a ready welcome.

Primary markets with their basic preferences (which are often waived for the unusual story) are:

True Detective Mysteries and *The Master Detective,* both issued by Macfadden Publications, 1926 Broadway, New York, and edited by John Shuttleworth. The requirements are identical, with T. D. M. being given preference of cases. Mr. Shuttleworth wants true detective crime stories written under an official's by-line in short stories of from 2,000 to 7,000 words and serials in installments of 6,000 to 7,000 words. These two books hold more closely to the out-and-out mystery story than their competitors. All stories must be accompanied by actual photographs or lists of available pictures. The rate of payment is $0.01 a word and upon acceptance with additional payment of from $1-$5 for photographs used. Mr. Shuttleworth will provide detailed instructions and case cards on request.

Real Detective, recently moved from Chicago to 1,300 Paramount Building, New York, under new ownership. West F. Peterson has succeeded Edwin Baird as editor and requires well written, striking, true illustrated crime stories and detective mystery short stories of lengths up to 7,000, and novelettes of varying lengths. Queries about proposed stories are welcomed. The payment is $0.01 to $0.02 a word on acceptance with $3 each for accepted photographs.

Startling Detective Adventures, 529 South 7th Street, Minneapolis, edited by Douglas Lurton, requires true, illustrated, crime stories and detective mysteries of a startling nature; shorts 1,000 to 5,000 words and serials in 4,000 word installments. Official by-lines are desirable but not imperative. Excellent photographs are required. Immediate queries on newly developing cases are appreciated. Case outline blanks and an instruction sheet will be mailed on receipt of stamped, addressed envelope. Payment is $0.01 a word and up on acceptance with a minimum of $3 additional for each accepted photograph. Prompt reports are assured.

Aside from these four primary and active markets there are a number of pulp paper mystery story magazines that occasionally publish true stories as variety.

Liberty magazine, Lincoln Square, New York, occasionally prints true crime mystery stories, generally by special arrangement with the writer.

The Blue Book magazine, 230 Park Avenue, New York, true experience contests are open to adventuresome true crime or mystery cases.

Mystery Magazine of the Tower group, 55 Fifth Avenue, New York, Occasionally uses true mysteries.

Real America, 1050 N. LaSalle Street, Chicago, edited by Edwin Baird, will publish exposes of graft and corruption and other crimes of a current nature dealing with vital problems.

Occasionally *True Confessions,* 529 South 7th Street, Minneapolis, prints true crime confessions of girls and women involved in the underworld when the cases involve love and emotion.

A nother formula that could be followed when writing fiction or "true" detective stories.

1.   Opening (choose one or more): A call for help and ensuing action, dramatic discovery of crime, visualization of the crime-in-progress, assignment of case to detective, or description of the scene (but usually wait until...).
2.   The setting: describing center target (usually a body) of scene and work your way out.
3.   The body: chasing down leads, discovering clues, making deductions...
4.   Climax: having held something exciting in mystery, reveal it.

WHY AREN'T YOUR DETECTIVE STORIES SELLING?

By Lurton Blassingame

This article originally appeared in the May 1933 issue of Writer's Digest. Blassingame was a writer himself, and went on to become the literary agent to Frank Herbert and Robert A Heinlein.

In the past ten days I have met three writers who, from one to two years ago, were making a comfortable living by writing action stories; today they are selling almost nothing. Two of these authors were writing gangster stories exclusively and the third was doing some copy for the gangster magazines; today the gangster magazines are as dead as their hundreds of fictional villains, and many of their authors, who have shown that they write well enough to sell, are going around like Cassius with a lean and hungry look.

"Why," I asked each of them, "don't you write detective stories?"

In each case the response was practically the same: The author's eyes narrowed, he looked at me to see if I was joking, and seeing I wasn't, said rather stiffly, "That's what I'm writing!"

Now I happen to know that the detective story magazines are very actively in the market for copy. The fad for the gangster story has passed, partly because public sentiment regarding Prohibition has changed and the purveyors of liquor are not generally looked upon as cloven-hoofed demons, partly because readers grew tired of having machine guns rattle on every page as one mob blasted down the members of another in the fiction which was so popular during the days when Prohibition was a "noble experiment." A different type of crime story was demanded and those writers who are keeping up with popular demand in the men's action field are supplying this demand at editorial rates which are quite adequate to keep them from joining the army of unemployment which Roosevelt plans to collect for reforestation work.

Before getting down to a serious shop talk discussion of what the editors are buying— and they are buying a quantity of it and looking for more—let's narrow our audience so we can be comfortable. We'll excuse both those misled writers who use singular verbs with plural nouns and those ambitious writers who are only interested in doing the big smooth paper story and the even more difficult and commendable story for the literary magazines; if you'll stand for a minute we'll even excuse most of the women, for few of them have the interest in, and the knowledge of, crime to make them successful competitors in the detective field.

Now we can be more comfortable and get our pipes going. There are left only a few girls, most of them with newspaper experience, and the remainder of you have either sold stories in the action field or have received letters about your rejected stories which let you know that you write well enough to sell and that you only need to get the right kind of plots to ring the editorial cash register.

All set? Good, let's go.

There are two types of detective stories selling steadily today —the kind which the editors call the "menace" yarn and the straight action-detective story. The old deductive detective story—in which the hero appears on the scene after the murder has occurred, finds a few clues, queries a few suspects, and then at the end points out the guilty man-is almost as extinct as the dodo. Once in a long time such a story will get by if very short, but if you have such stories on hand you probably will waste postage in sending them out and you certainly should not write them. A few gangsters are still alive despite the tons of lead through which they have passed in recent years, but most of the gangster magazines have been buried in Potter's Field, and if you are still writing the straight gangster story or even the story in which the detective hero goes up against the bootlegging and dope running gangs you have no one but yourself to blame for rejection slips. Even the story of the criminal who sets out to commit the perfect crime and at the end is captured through some step which he felt sure would insure his success or his escape is now in the bread line. *Dime Detective, Black Mask, Clues,* and *Shadow* are all against him and such a story must be unusually well done to get by with the other magazines. Let's avoid this type.

There is an unusually good market today for the well written story of menace. If this word does not give you a clear picture of the type of fiction desired, I suggest that you read "The Phantom of the Opera" and the adventure of Sherlock Holmes in which he uncovers "The Hound of the Baskervilles." Then to get a little closer to the present, reread Sax Rohmer's "Fu Manchu" and you will be ready to read current magazines with a full understanding of what editors mean when they speak of "menace." In this type of story some person or thing hangs a veil of horror over the characters in the story; we never know when this "menace" will strike, but we do know it will continue to commit depredations until the hero does his stuff and overcomes it in the final climax. "Dracula" was a menace play.

I see that the man sitting by the fireplace, the chap who looks like Lincoln and who has finished his second stein of beer, evidently has something on his mind. What's that? Yes, you are quite right—there is a difference in "The Hound of the Baskervilles" and in "Fu Manchu." These two stories represent the two tendencies in the "menace" fiction being published today.

In "The Hound of the Baskervilles" we do not know who is committing the crimes or why; so in addition to the menace there is also a mystery. Sax Rohmer, however, lets us know the identity of his criminal, but the monster Fu Manchu is too clever to be captured and continues to commit his crimes despite all the efforts of the police to apprehend him.

Now let's come down to the present and see examples of these different types of stories in the current magazines. We can find an excellent example of the mystery menace in T. T. Flynn's "Five Doomed Men" in Dime Detective. (This magazine uses only novelettes between ten and twenty five thousand words so don't waste your postage and the editor's time by sending him short stories.)

Flynn opens his story in a newspaper office with the hero, a reporter, being asked by the office boy to help get rid of "a nut" who is in the waiting room to see the boss. The hero goes out and talks to a little foreigner who is evidently ill from lack of food. And the little foreigner, his eyes glazed with terror, tells the hero how from his basement room he has looked across an alley and watched a giant ape-thing hang poised on a fire escape ladder until some man has passed underneath when the ape-thing dropped on the man, broke his neck silently, threw the victim's body over his shoulder and stalked off into the darkness.

When he has finished telling his story, the little man faints and is taken to a hospital where he dies of malnutrition without giving his address. The hero thinks the man was telling some story born of a distorted mind but that night he, himself, runs into the "ape-thing." He has been sent by the editor of the paper ostensibly to cover a social gathering but in reality to get dope on a big politician. He has slipped away from the dancing to see what he could find in the host's home office when the ape-thing comes through the window and attacks him. He fights but is helpless and is knocked out. He comes to in the room and finds that the safe has been looted and the owner of the house, his neck broken, is lying nearby!

The hero is suspected by the police and is taken to jail as a material witness. The editor gets him out and the two of them go to see another partner of the man who has been killed. They find the ape-thing in the house but it escapes and kills the partner as he drives up out front. This time, however, the others have seen the ape-thing and the hero is not suspected.

There had been five partners in the firm with which the murdered men were associated; three are left. The hero, posing as a crook, traps one of the partners into admitting crooked work and thus is trapped by some of this man's henchmen. He is almost killed but manages to make his escape. Investigating and following up all clues, he finds a room where the criminal who is committing crimes disguised as the ape-thing is evidently hiding out on occasion. When another of the partners is killed, the murderer is almost trapped and the hero manages to wound him. The hero leads the police to the secret hangout and they are on hand when the crook arrives. In a desperate fight he is killed and turns out to be the fifth partner.

There are logical explanations of why he turned on the others and the story is cleared up satisfactorily.

Notice carefully the technique used in plotting this story. First, we are given some hint of the mystery, something which sounds impossible and fantastic and which holds a note of horror. The hero immediately goes into action against this menace, getting himself into and out of danger as he approaches closer to a solution. Then the story winds up in a good action scene which also makes everything which has happened logical and explains away the apparent impossibilities seen earlier.

The place where most beginners slip up in handling the menace type of story is in their failure to make all of the action logical. In looking over rejected stories recently in editorial offices I have found that there are two big reasons for rejection among the writers who have turned out this type of story. The first, of course, is the failure of the author to write well enough. A number of writers waste their time and money in producing and sending out stories which do not have a page without some mistake in sentence structure or spelling. Such persons have no business writing short stories and we've ruled them out of our audience.

The second big group of writers meeting with failure in this field are those with sufficient education but who follow their imagination where it leads, caring nothing for the probabilities and consistencies necessary to make a story convincing. A typical rejected story which I saw recently dealt with a "menace" which destroyed Indians and travelers on a western desert. At the end it was revealed that this supposed Desert God was in reality a white man in charge of a band of international jewel thieves. The author was quite right in explaining away the menace and making it a real human being—but he forgot that international jewel thieves don't operate in deserts where there are but a few simple Indians and an occasional traveller! He also let his hero, a college man, believe in one paragraph that the menace was some inhuman monster, in the next paragraph the hero didn't believe, and in the third he believed again! Net result—the editors didn't believe in him or the story and another rejection slip went out.

In the current issue of *Ten Detective Aces* Lester Dent has a mystery-menace story where the criminal does not disguise himself as something fantastic, but succeeds in spreading terror and death through his cleverness. At the end he is revealed by the hero as a private detective who was brought on the scene to protect the owner of vast wealth and who decided that he would kill off all the persons concerned and keep the wealth for himself. It doesn't make any difference to the editors whether you use a disguised menace or not; your menace must be kept logical whether he uses a disguise or whether he simply gets by in his own character and dress.

The second type of menace story is the one in which the menace is known but still presents a serious obstacle, increasing his insidious influence until he is finally overthrown by the hero. Arthur J. Burks has a story of this kind in the current issue of *All Detective*. He tells us about Dorus Noel, a young American who spent some years in China where he came into conflict with the master criminal of all North China— Chu Chul. Dorus, thinking he has disposed of Chu Chul in China, is now operating in New York's Chinatown. When the story opens he is expecting his Chinese servant to summon him to dinner but instead he hears the servant playing on the five-noted flute. He goes to the kitchen and finds the man under the influence of a drug administered by Chu Chul. Dorus helps the boy escape the effects of the drug, but a short time later the servant is killed by one of Chu Chul's men. Dorus tries to locate Chu Chul but cannot and discovers that the man already has his influence over Chinatown and has the entire section afraid of him. The only way the hero can reach the villain is to permit himself to be captured, for he knows that Chu Chul will not kill him before gloating over him. Dorus is captured and is taken before Chu Chul, but through his knowledge of jiu-jitsu, he not only defends himself against the villain's henchmen but sets fire to the villain. When Chu Chul attempts to escape Noel follows and so gets away from the henchmen. Chu Chul is seriously injured if not dead and for the time being the hero is free and victorious.

Do you see the difference in the technique and plotting of this story and the one of Flynn's mentioned above? Instead of the villain being a mystery, he is known but is none the less powerful. The hero pursues him but loses until the climax when he finally wins out. I suppose it is needless to point out that you do not need an Oriental in the role of the villain; I have seen very good stories of this kind in which the villain took various roles from that of a man about town who is respected in social circles and on whom the hero can get no real evidence to the old fashioned gang leader who gags witnesses against him with lead. Unless you know a little about the Orient and Orientals it is better not to use a Chinaman for a villain. Burks used one effectively in this story but he spent some years in

Peking and he is, I know, very much at home in New York's Chinatown.

In looking through rejected stories of this kind I found many which failed to succeed, not because they were not sufficiently well written, but because the authors had not made it convincing that the villain could not be captured until the end. If your hero is going to be a stubborn blockhead who will not take care of himself and who will not present evidence to the authorities when he has it, you can't expect him to be greatly admired by the readers, and consequently the editors do not let such stories see print.

We come now to the second big type of detective stories being bought today—the straight action-detective yarn. *The Shadow* is one of the several magazines which offers a good market for this type of story. In the issue before me Winston Bouve has an excellent example of the kind of story which sells in this field.

His hero, a detective sergeant named Corcoran, is off duty and is dozing in his room, He awakens to see, in the room just across the apartment house court from his, a small man sitting in a chair and stabbed to death! Corcoran rushes downstairs and discovers from the doorman that no one has gone out the front and from a woman across the street that no one has come out the side entrance. He has the place surrounded by detectives and leads the way to the murdered man's apartment. Entering it he finds it empty! His brother officers believe Corcoran has been seeing things until he discovers a spot of blood. By a quick bit of detective work and a telephone call to headquarters, he finds the victim is a former criminal just out of prison and that he has sworn to get two other crooks who double-crossed him and had him sent up. Corcoran concludes that the body could only have been moved by way of the dumbwaiter and a tiny bit of evidence sends him to another apartment above the one in which the crook had been living. There are apparently only a man and his wife in the apartment but the hero's eagle eye discovers the place hasn't been kept as a woman would keep it and he manages, despite the objections of the man and his supposed wife, to discover the dead body.

This starts the fireworks, for the woman proves to be a man and Corcoran is attacked. The crooks almost escape but Corcoran follows and shoots them down in a gun battle. Within an hour after he has awakened and seen the body he has discovered the crooks and brought them to book.

Observe this technique carefully. The story opens with an attention arresting scene; the hero goes into action at once, and though he is thwarted and laughed at for a time, he comes through victorious in a stirring action climax.

Contrast this with another rejected story. It was better written than Bouve's and in it the hero was also but a few feet away when murder occurred. But there the similarity ended. For 6,000 words the hero looked over the scene of the crime and questioned suspects; then he arrested the guilty man.

No action here, no thrilling scenes. And a story 1,000 words too long. For with the magazines getting thinner, stories of 2,000 to 5,000 words sell when yarns of more than 5,000 words-unless they are strong novelettes—are a drug on the market.

Let's take another example of the action-detective story, this time a yarn from *Black Mask* by William Rollins, Jr., called "*Kayo And The Killers.*"

A friend of the hero's goes to see a politician who is running for district attorney. When the friend doesn't return the hero telephones the politician's home and is talking to the boy when the connection is broken. The hero goes out to investigate, slips in, and is captured in the house by the politician but escapes when he manages to turn off the lights. When the friend's body is discovered the next day the hero examines it and then goes to the present district attorney and tells him the murder was committed in the house of his political opponent and that he, the hero, is going to get evidence against the guilty man. He tells the district attorney where he is living. After escaping an attack at his room he goes back to the home of the man who is a candidate for the district attorney's office, captures and binds him, and telephones the prosecuting attorney telling him where he is and what he has done. The hero then begins to search for certain evidence he wants but the house is entered by two gunmen who attempt to kill him. The hero kills one and captures the other and when the prosecuting attorney and the detectives come out ready to arrest the politician whom the hero has captured earlier the hero points out that it is the present district attorney who is guilty. He knows this because he was attacked in his room—and no one knew where he lived but the district attorney—and he was attacked at the home of the politician when the district attorney and the politician were the only two who knew he was there. The captured gunman has already signed a confession in the hope of obtaining leniency.

The story moves swiftly from beginning to end, the hero is in danger, but the entire story is perfectly logical despite the big surprise at the end.

I have known writers who have sold more than a hundred stories of gangsters to fall down in writing the detective story because they did not make their heroes cleverer than their criminals. Recently I saw a rejected manuscript in an editors office in which the hero, after having run around throughout the entire story on the trail of the person he thought was the criminal, was told at the end of the story-after he had shot the criminal by mistake !—that he had really killed the guilty man! Instead of the hero solving the story and being brighter than everyone else, everyone seemed to know the solution instead of the hero.

The author of this story had sold dozens of stories in different fields but when he tackled the detective story he failed to understand the principles back of successful writing before he began work. The result was failure for him in a field when he should have met with success.

In a brief talk like this I can't hope to give you all the points necessary for success but I have tried to outline the things you should look for in your reading of the magazines. Never send out any stories until you have read and carefully studied several issues of the magazines to which you intend to submit manuscripts. Then, when your stories are written, make sure that they are as well written and as well plotted, though original, as the stories which the editors are buying.

Here is a brief summary which will guide you in your reading.

If you wish to write the menace story, read *Dime Detective* (but remember it uses only novelettes between 10,000 and 25,000 words) and *Ten Detective Aces*. This latter market uses short stories between 1,000 and 15,000 words. In the novelettes a little pseudo-science is permissible.

You will also find occasional mystery-menace stories in *Clues, All Detective* and *Detective Fiction Weekly,* though these three markets use more detective-action than menace stories. Shorts should be between 1,000 and 5,000. *Ten Detective Aces* uses some action-detective stories, though it prefers the menace yarn.

Shadow and *Detective Fiction Weekly* buy more detective action stories than they do mystery-menace yarns and the detective-action story is bought almost exclusively by *Black Mask*. For this latter market you must write very well indeed and in the objective style made popular in the detective field by Dashiel Hammett.

There are other markets for the detective story but I've mentioned only the more active ones. Remember that if you send in a poorly written and poorly plotted story you will not only get it back but you will prejudice editors against your work. If you send in well written and well plotted stories which show you have been studying the magazine and are capable of producing work which meets the standard set by the editors, you will meet with a very cordial reception.

And now I move that the meeting be adjourned. It's late enough for murder to stalk the streets and so it's time we were trailing the menacing shadows of evil to their lairs. There's good safe money in murder—if its done by typing on white paper and the villain is finally overcome.

The lesson here is to study your market. You can do that if you are trying to get traditionally published by reading a few things that publisher has picked up. If you are planning on self-publishing, then check out what is selling best in your genre on Amazon.

IS THE ATTIC TRUNK YOUR GOAL?

By G. Ernest Hill

This article is from the December 1930 issue of Writers Markets and Methods.

This is going to be a frank but friendly chat with readers of *Markets and Methods* — an attempt to change the *I-would-like* consciousness which so many of us are holding to the *I-will* consciousness which every writer needs if he is to write to sell.

I am prompted to enter into this discussion because of a recent conversation I had with a young man who has been half-heartedly trying to write for some time, but without other success than the self-satisfaction of having tried. He came to see me about his writing, and to ascertain if he possessed ability worth his time and effort to develop.

"Of course," he said by way of introducing the subject, "I do not expect to sell anything; I just want to write for the satisfaction it gives me."

"Have you any conscientious objections to selling what you write?" I inquired.

"Oh, no," he replied, a bit embarrassed, I thought, "but I don't think I could ever write anything worthy of publication."

Could anything be more asinine?

It developed that this gentleman was a specialist in his own line-child welfare—and held a responsible civil service position in a large Western city. His work was highly constructive, educative and corrective. Although a young man in his thirties, his activities with juvenile delinquents had already attracted national attention, and he was well on the way to become a recognized authority.

And this man did not believe that he could ever write anything worthy of publication!

"Life Laughs"—we were told editorially last month in *Markets and Methods*. Surely, life must laugh at our foolish gestures of modesty—our inane attempts at self-kidding.

The gentleman I speak of has a splendid background of education and experience; he has a real message that the world is waiting to receive; all he needs is a bit of coaching in the professional technique of selection, arrangement and presentation of material to enable him to deliver his message in a fashion acceptable to editors. And when pinned down to a pointed question, he admitted that he would like to see his ideas in print. His remark about soul satisfaction was only a gesture—an affectation. He believes in the Law of Compensation, which declares that a job well done is always worth its price.

"Life Laughs"—and gives us just what we demand of it—no more, no less. We must expect abundantly if we are to receive abundantly. Philosophers tell us that "he gets most who gives most," and I believe it. But the giving without the expectation of receiving is a lifeless gift that lacks normal incentive and the vital, virile, magnetic quality of attraction.

Desire is the self-starter that cranks the motor of action. Without desire there would be no Universe—just a void of vast nothingness. Desire keeps the planets whirling in their orbits. Desire operates the Laws of Nature. It is a creative as well a motivating force; it induces action and presupposes realization. In Desire the element of selfishness is incapable—nor should we try to escape it. We are not Himalayan ascetics, living to a creed of desirelessness and selflessness. The philosophy of self-realization may be engulfed in Occidental egoism, but it gets somewhere and fills human needs.

I would not have readers of *Markets and Methods* conclude that I am propounding a doctrine of pure commercialism to be applied to the God-given art of authorship. Nothing could be farther from my purpose. Leave the monetary returns out of this consideration, if you choose, and view it wholly from the viewpoint of accomplishment—that is, getting something done. Evaluate whatever talent you may have and make of it a producer that accomplishes something.

Of what avail are a thousand manuscripts in the attic trunk if they have accomplished nothing but to satisfy the creative urge?

Justify that urge within you for the divine spark that it is. Let is perform its perfect work, however imperfect the instrumentality may be, for the instrument can be made perfect.

There are various reasons why many would-be writers remain would-be's—reasons that have nothing to do with literary technique. A bit of self-analysis may, perhaps, determine what is holding one back.

Fear is one of these reasons—fear of being turned down, of making a mistake. How many brilliant ideas have been buried alive in the grave of inhibited hopes which fear alone has dug. We forget that some of the greatest achievements have grown out of the greatest errors. But the most insidious stumbling block, in my opinion, is this exaggerated humility that takes on the affectation of modesty. In nine cases out of ten such a gesture is merely a bid for approbation, and is defeated by its very obviousness.

Try as you will, you cannot really kid yourself, because you know your own desires and motives. The attempt to do so in itself has a retarding influence. Thought is force, and operates in the direction liberated. The same force, concentrated upon our honest motives, is certain to result in definite progress.

Be honest with yourself. If you are writing, with the attic trunk as your goal, don't waste time on methods. But if the printed page or the audible screen constitute your objective, expect to win—and YOU WILL!

And be forewarned: *Editors pay for what they use!*

So, this article could have done with a few examples of authors who just kept writing and learning until they "made it." It is a little reminiscent of the lectures I would receive as a child when my dad would tell me why I just needed to try harder.

However, I think it does ask a very important question: **What is your goal with writing?** Are you seriously just writing so that your words can sit on your hard drive for a few years until your hard drive crashes and they are gone forever? Or do you desperately want to share your stories and entertain whoever you can? If you want the latter, you *have* to pay the price: study and practice the craft.

About the Editor

Bryce is a huge fan of the classic pulps, enough that he started one of his own. It's called StoryHack Action & Adventure. Check it out at StoryHack.com

Made in the USA
Columbia, SC
21 November 2018